Gary R. Gruber's
Inside
Strategies
for the
S·A·T

by Gary R. Gruber, Ph.D.

EDUCATIONAL DESIGN, INC.   **EDI 390**

47 WEST 13 STREET, NEW YORK, NY 10011

The first three sample reading comprehension passages and associated questions on pp. 140–141 are selected from **5 SATs**. Copyright ©1981 by College Entrance Examination Board and Educational Testing Service. Reprinted by permission of Educational Testing Service, copyright owner of the sample questions.

Permission to reprint the above sample SAT material does not constitute review or endorsement by Educational Testing Service or the College Board of this publication as a whole or of any other sample questions or testing information it may contain.

ISBN# 0-87694-234-6   EDI 390
Printed in the United States of America

TABLE OF CONTENTS

BEFORE YOU BEGIN...

Are you worried about taking the Scholastic Aptitude Tests? Just about everybody who has to take them is. Nevertheless, it's a fact of college life: if you want to get into a really good college of your choice, you have to score well on your SAT's.

This book is designed to help you improve your SAT scores. It contains over 60 of the most powerful strategies and shortcuts for answering questions on the SAT -- or, for that matter, on any similar standardized test.

These strategies really work!

In a test of the method taught in this book, a broad sampling of students was given an SAT exam under strict exam conditions. The students then studied and practiced the strategies taught in this book for between 15 and 30 hours. Each student then took a second SAT exam.

Comparison of before-and-after test scores showed that the students had made amazing gains in their ability to handle SAT questions. The average gain was 133 points -- perhaps the highest in the nation. Half the students involved in the test gained between 133 and 300 points!

Why do the strategies in this book work? Because the testmakers who write the SAT questions actually design about half of the questions to be solved in two different ways -- a long way, and a short way using the strategic methods taught in this book!

Here's an SAT-type example -- one we'll use again later in the book. Which of the following two quantities is larger

-- the fraction 6/13, or the difference between the two fractions 7/12 and 1/13? If you work the problem the long way, subtracting 1/13 from 7/12 and comparing the answer with 6/13, it may take you several minutes to get an answer. If you use the strategy taught in this book, it will take you approximately 5 seconds. (If you can't wait to find out how it's done, turn to Strategy 33 in the book.)

<u>Now here's an important word of caution.</u> The questions in some other books that prepare you for the SAT are not always designed like the actual SAT questions. And so, they cannot be solved the same way as actual SAT questions, using SAT-type strategies and shortcuts. This book uses the real SAT problem-solving methods, developed after 20 years of research and after critical analysis of thousands of actual SAT questions.

So let's get right down to increasing your SAT score. Look over the Table of Contents so that you understand how the book is organized. Then work your way through the book, chapter by chapter and strategy by strategy. Take your time, but make sure you really understand each strategy before you go on to the next. Review frequently, and review each chapter as a whole after you finish it.

Remember, each strategy or shortcut that you can use to answer a question on the SAT will raise your score about 10 points. So the more you understand and remember, the more you will raise your SAT score.

Good luck with your SAT's!

Gary R. Gruber

WHAT'S ON THE SAT?

The SAT contains <u>two math</u> sections and <u>two verbal</u> sections (30 minutes for each section) which <u>count</u> toward your SAT score. The other two sections (also 30 minutes each in length) <u>do not</u> count toward your SAT score. One of these non-counted sections will be either a math, verbal, or grammar section and the other section will be a grammar section. One grammar section (there's usually only one on each SAT) <u>does not count toward the SAT score</u> and is only used for English placement in college. Research shows that <u>it is not a good idea to study for this grammar section</u> because you do not want to be placed in a higher position in your English classes for which you do not honestly qualify, because you will not be able to keep up with the work in those classes. The other section, which also does not count toward your SAT score, is experimental and used for SAT pretesting of new items. So there are <u>four</u> of the <u>six</u> sections (two in math and two in verbal-not grammar) which you must be concerned about.

THE VERBAL SECTIONS

The verbal sections contain antonyms (a total of 25 which count), sentence completions (15 which count), analogies (20 which count), and reading comprehension (5 or 6 passages -25 questions which count).

THE MATH SECTIONS

There are two types of math questions. The regular multiple-choice (a total of 40 which count) and the quantitative comparison type (20 which count).

A TYPICAL FORMAT OF AN SAT (The order may vary from test to test).

Section	Question-Type	No. Questions	Time Limit
1	VERBAL	45	30 minutes
	Antonyms	15	
	Analogies	10	
	Sentence Completions	10	
	Reading Comprehension (2 passages)	10	
2	MATH	35	30 minutes
	Regular	15	
	Quantitative Comparison	20	
3	VERBAL	40	30 minutes
	Antonyms	10	
	Sentence Completions	5	
	Analogies	10	
	Reading Comprehension (3 or 4 passages)	15	
4	TEST OF STANDARD WRITTEN ENGLISH (GRAMMAR)-doesn't count toward SAT score	50	30 minutes
5	MATH	25	30 minutes
	Regular	25	
6	VERBAL, MATH OR GRAMMAR- Experimental-doesn't count toward any score.	varies	30 minutes

GENERAL STRATEGIES

STRATEGY 1

Know the directions for all question types ahead of time.

Memorize all the directions given in this book for each question type (analogies, sentence completions, quantitative comparisons, etc.) <u>so that you don't have to refer to those directions on your actual exam</u>. Don't waste any time doing sample questions on your test -- get right into the actual SAT questions on your test. Some students say, "Well, what if the SAT people give synonyms instead of antonyms?" Believe me, that will never happen unless the SAT people give you and me ample notice in their SAT bulletin. It is extremely unlikely that the SAT will be changed for many years to come.

STRATEGY 2

Memorize the following average answering times.

Below is a table that shows the <u>average</u> times you should spend on questions in the different sections of the SAT:

Section	Average time per question
Antonyms	20 sec.
Sentence Completion	40 sec.
Analogies	30 sec.
Reading Comprehension	
passage with 3 questions	4 min. (total)
4 questions	5 min. (total)
5 questions	6 min. (total)
6 questions	7 min. (total)
7 questions	9 min. (total)
Regular Math	72 sec.
Quantitative Comparisons	36 sec.

8

Memorize these average times and use them to pace your-self when you take the test. If you have not decided on an approach to a question after <u>half</u> its average time is up, guess rapidly and go on to the next question.

STRATEGY 3

It's OK to guess.

Even if you have no idea how to answer a question, and even though you are penalized for guessing wrong, (you get ¼ point deduction for 5-choice questions and 1/3 point deduction for 4-choice questions), <u>it is wise not to leave the answer blank</u>. A blank space opens up the possibility of mismarking your answer sheet. Furthermore, I can show you a convincing argument for guessing, if you can't answer the question otherwise.

Suppose that you have 5 five-choice questions:

```
1.  (A) ... (B) ... (C) ... (D) ... (E)
2.  (A) ... (B) ... (C) ... (D) ... (E)
3.  (A) ... (B) ... (C) ... (D) ... (E)
4.  (A) ... (B) ... (C) ... (D) ... (E)
5.  (A) ... (B) ... (C) ... (D) ... (E)
```

The chance of getting <u>only 1</u> of the five questions right by blind guessing is pretty much 100%. Suppose you are unlucky and get all the other four questions wrong. You would get +1 for getting one question right and -¼ X 4 for getting four questions wrong. (The penalty is ¼ point for wrong answers.). +1 -(¼ X 4) = +1 -1 = 0. Therefore, if you were unlucky and got only one question right and the other four wrong, you would still break even and not really lose by guessing! That is, you'd end up with 0, as if you left <u>all</u> the answers blank. So my suggestion to you would be to always guess <u>if you can't figure out how to answer the question</u>. Of course, I'll show you how to make some very sophisticated guesses later on.

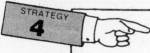

If two choices look equally good, guess and go on.

If you have narrowed all the choices down to a choice between two answers but cannot decide between them, just pick one of the two at random. Don't waste time! Go on to the next question. This way you will not psychologically exhaust yourself trying to pick the correct answer. Research shows that it is psychologically better for you to actually get the previous question wrong, rather than to always wonder whether you should go back and change the answer.

Beware of answers with clues that seem too obvious.

Look out for answers that seem at first glance to contain very obvious clues. These answers may be a special kind of trap designed to lead you into making a wrong guess.

Here's an example. A question asks you to find a pair of words related to each other in the same way as SUBMARINE and SHARK. Among the choices are the pair subway and tiger. Look out! This choice is a trap! The prefix sub- in subway is designed to make you think of the sub- in submarine. And both a tiger and a shark are fierce meat-eaters. But look again. A subway and a tiger are not really related to each other in any clear way at all! The "obvious clues" are designed to lead you away from the correct choice -- airplane and eagle. (A submarine is an underwater vehicle, a shark is an underwater meat-eater; an airplane is a flying vehicle, an eagle is a flying meat-eater.)

The "too-obvious clues" answers can trap you in two ways. They can trap you if you really don't now an answer and have to guess. And they can trap you if you are going too fast and get careless. You may choose the answer with the "too-obvious clue" and miss a correct answer that you would have gotten if you hadn't been going so fast.

Try logic before you try guessing.

If you don't know the meaning of a word, you may be able to figure it out <u>by pure logic</u>! Here's an example: Suppose you have the analogy: LIAR: MENDACIOUS (with five choices for the corresponding analogy). Many people would say if you don't know the meaning of MENDACIOUS, don't try to answer the question. But look -- MENDACIOUS has the form of an adjective, so it probably describes either the word LIAR or its opposite. (Actually, the word MENDACIOUS means "lying.") This kind of logical deduction can be of great help on the SAT. More about it later.

Look out for traps.

Whatever you do, <u>never rush into getting answers</u>. They will probably be wrong answers. When you rush into getting an answer and have not critically thought the solution out, work from Choice E to Choice A. That is, don't look at Choice A first, but look at Choice E and work backwards from the choices. Here's an example of how you may be lured into an incorrect answer:

If $x + y = 6$ and $xy = 5$, what is $x^2 + y^2$?
(A) 36 (B) 25 (C) 31 (D) 11 (E) 26

Here you may have thought that $(x + y)^2 = x^2 + y^2$ and got the answer 6 X 6 = 36 (Choice A). Or you may have wanted to multiply xy by xy to get 5 X 5= 25, etc. What you really have to know is how to obtain the quantity $x^2 + y^2$ from $x+y$ and from xy. The answer is Choice E. I'll show you how to get that answer <u>without</u> having to solve for x and y, later.

If you have to try all the choices, start with Choice E.

Here's an example:

> If x is an integer, which number is sometimes even?
>
> (A) $2x + 1$ (B) $2x - 1$ (C) $4x - 1$
> (D) $3(2x + 1)$ (E) $(x + 1)^2$

Many students would try different numbers for x and substitute those numbers in each of the choices. That's o.k. But the student would start with Choice A first! Take my advice and start with the Choice E first, then try Choice D etc. Let's try a simple number for x like x = 1. You can see that substituting x = 1 in Choice E, you get $(1 + 1)^2 = 2^2 = 4$. 4 is even so Choice E is correct. No need to work on the other choices!

So, for questions where one usually has to test out all the choices and eliminate the incorrect ones, the test-maker usually has as an answer Choice E or Choice D. This is because the test-maker wants to test to see if the student is able to eliminate all or most of the incorrect choices before arriving at the correct one. And since most students usually start with Choice A then try Choice B, etc., the test-maker puts the correct choice at the end of the choices.

A word of warning: This strategy works only in the special circumstance when a question cannot be answered without looking at all the choices. For example, you would not use it to find the answer to a question like this:

> If x = 5, what is x^2 + 3?
>
> (A) 8   (B) 13   (C) 28   (D) 30   (E) 45

In this question, you do not need to look at the choices at all to get the correct answer. You would first calculate that x^2 + 3 = 28, and only then go to the choices to find which one is the same as your answer. So the strategy does not apply.

A second warning: The strategy of starting with Choice E is not designed to give you the correct answer by itself. It is designed to help you find the correct answer faster when you start working through the choices.

VERBAL STRATEGIES

ANTONYMS

The first verbal section of an SAT is usually an Antonyms section, where you are given a word and asked to find its opposite. Here's a very simple example:

```
STRONG :        (A) thin
                (B) weak
                (C) little
                (D) blue
                (E) wrong
```

Since the opposite of STRONG is <u>weak</u>, you would mark Choice B.

The Antonyms section of the SAT is primarily a test of your vocabulary. So this chapter is designed to give you strategies to try whenever you are uncertain of the meaning of a word.

STRATEGY
9

Learn these special lists of words, roots, and prefixes.

A computer analysis of the Antonyms section in 33 recent SAT exams (over 5,000 questions) yielded the following key list of words. Most of these have appeared more than once on the SATs. (The paired words are so closely related that they might as well be a single repeated word.) After each word is a number showing the number of times it has appeared. You may wish to make sure that you know the meanings of these words.

We have not given you the definitions of these words. We found that you learn better if you look up the meanings in the dictionary yourself. That way, you'll retain the meanings better, since you are doing the work, and I am not spoon-feeding you.

Look carefully at the list. Check any words whose meanings you are not sure of. Then look them up in the dictionary. Be sure to write down the definition of each word you look up.

abolish 2
accolade 2
acquiesce 2
amass 2
ambulatory 2
ameliorate 2
amity 2
atrophy 2
bizarre 2
blunder 2
burgeon 2
capricious 4
clemency 2
[coalesce 2
[coalescence 1
[compress 1
[compression 1
[confide 1
[confidential 1
confound 2
congeal 2
[contaminant 1
[contaminate 2
converge 2
copious 2
corrugated 2
[corrupt 1
[corruption 1
daunt 2
debilitate 2
deplete 2

disentangle 2
[disputatious 1
[dispute 2
efface 3
enhance 2
ephemeral 3
[euphonious 1
[euphony 1
[expedite 1
[expeditious 1
facilitate 2
fallow 2
fertile 2
[flourish 3
[flower 1
fraudulent 2
garner 2
guile 2
hackneyed 2
hefty 2
hideous 2
innocuous 2
irascible 2
kindle 2
[leniency 1
[lenient 1
mitigate 2
munificent 2
parsimony 2
paucity 2

[peripheral 2
[periphery 2
premature 2
premeditated 2
proclivity 2
[prodigal 1
[prodigious 2
[profuse 1
[profusion 2
recalcitrant 2
recant 2
rescind 2
reserve 2
saccharine 2
squander 2
subtle 2
summary 2
summon 2
sumptuous 2
[surreptitious 1
[surreptitiously 1
[tenacious 1
[tenacity 1
[transience 1
[transient 1
turbulence 2
venturesome 2
viable 2
vilification 2
zany 2

Is there a short cut way to learn vocabulary? Well, there certainly is a more efficient way to learn the meaning of words than memorizing a word list. The SAT chooses words from a list of over 30,000.

Did you know that a reliable study has shown that <u>20 prefixes and 14 roots can help you to get the meaning of over 100,000 words?</u> Well, here are those roots and prefixes, and one or two more:

ROOT	MEANING	EXAMPLE
act, ag	do, act	activity, agent
apert	open	aperture
bas	low	basement
cap, capt	take, seize	capable, capture
ced, cess	give in, go	concede, recession
cred	believe	credible
curr, curs	run	current, precursor
dict	speak	dictionary, predict
duc, duct	lead	induce, conduct
equ	equal	equality, equanimity
fac, fact	make, do	facile, artifact
fer	bear, carry	offer, confer
graph	write	monograph, graphite
log	word, study of	dialog, biology
mitt, miss	send	permit, admission
par	equal	parity, disparate
plic	fold	complicated
pon	put, place	component
scrib, script	write	transcribe, subscription
sequ, secu	follow	sequel, consecutive
spec, spect	see	specimen, aspect
sto, stat, sisto,	stand, cause to stand	statue, insist
tact	touch	contact, tactile
ten	hold	retentive, tenacious
tend, tent, tens	stretch	extend, tension
un, uni	one	unilateral, unanimous
ven, vent	come	convenient, advent
ver	true	verify

PREFIX	MEANING	EXAMPLE
a,ab,abs	away, from	absent, abstinent
ad,a,ac,af, ag,an,ar,at,as	to, toward	adhere, annex, accede, adapt
bi,bis	two	biped, bicycle
circum	around	circumference, circumlocution
com,con	together, with	combination, connect
de	opposite, from	detract, demerit
dis,dif,di	apart	disperse, difference
epi	upon, on top of	epilogue
equi	equal	equality, equitable
ex, ef, e	out, from	eject, exalt, exit
in (en)	in, into	inject, endure
mal, male	bad, ill	malpractice, malevolent
mis	wrong	misplace, misunderstand
mono	alone, one, single	monotone, monopoly
non	not	nonsense
ob	in front, against	obviate, obvious
omni	everywhere, all	omnipresent, omnipotent
per	through	perceive, pervade
poly	many	polygon
post	after	posterior, postpone
pre	before	precursory, preface
pro	forward	proceed, promote
re	again	recall, recede
se	apart	secede
sub	under	subliminal, subway
super	greater, beyond	supernatural, superstition
trans	across	transpire, transcontinental
un,uni	one	unilateral, unity
un(pronounced uhn)	not	unethical

You will find that this list will be of considerable help in getting at the meaning of words. For example, take the word DISPARITY. If you remember what the list tells you -- that PAR means _equal_ and DIS means apart--you can reason that DISPARITY means _dissimilarity_ or _difference_.

Now try using the information in the list to get the answers to some typical SAT antonym questions. (Remember that in antonym-type questions, you are asked to find the word that expresses the opposite meaning to the given word.) Try them:

1. PRECURSORY
    (A) succeeding
    (B) flamboyant
    (C) cautious
    (D) simple
    (E) cheap

2. TENACIOUS
    (A) smooth
    (B) careful
    (C) fickle
    (D) argumentative
    (E) polite

3. CIRCUMVENT
    (A) to go the straight route
    (B) alleviate
    (C) to prey on ones emotions
    (D) scintillate
    (E) perceive correctly

4. MALEDICTION
    (A) sloppiness
    (B) praise
    (C) health
    (D) religiousness
    (E) proof

Knowing the prefix or root or both of the given word, you should be able to zero in on the correct opposite without mulling over the incorrect choices. In 1, you should know that PRE means before and CURS means to run. Therefore, PRECURSORY must mean to run before; so the opposite would be SUCCEEDING, Choice A. In 2, TEN means to hold, so TENACIOUS means persistent, and the opposite would be FICKLE, Choice C. In 3, CIRCUM means around. And, VENT means come, so CIRCUMVENT must mean to come around. The opposite would be to go the straight route, Choice A. In 4, MAL means ill or bad. DICT means speak. So, MALEDICTION must mean something that speaks ill of someone. The opposite would be praise, Choice B.

Notice how this method of knowing prefixes and roots helps you to zero in on the right choice. On the other hand, if you do not know how to get the meaning of a word by its prefix or root and you are not familiar with the word, you might as well guess immediately and then go on to the next question. Remember, do not try to psych out the test-maker or waste time mulling over a word! And remember, if you're not sure which of two or three choices is correct, just choose one of them at random—don't mull over which of the one or two or three choices is correct. You can always go back to the question later if you have time. The time you may spend mulling over choices will take valuable time away from you, time which you may be able to use to get many more questions right. Also, by mulling over a question, you will be put at a psychological disadvantage. You will be kept from looking freshly at upcoming questions, and you will always be wondering whether you made the right choice in the preceding question. This unfortunate situation can psychologically exhaust you for the rest of the exam.

The following strategy shows you how to combine the PREFIXES and ROOTS with a particularly useful approach:

Use the +, −, or 0 method.

Many times you can answer an antonym question by assigning to the parts of the words the signs +, − or 0. This is what I mean. Suppose you have the following SAT antonym question:

DISHEARTEN	(A) engage
	(B) encourage
	(C) predict
	(D) dismember
	(E) misinform

Since DIS means apart or against and has a <u>negative</u> connotation, and since HEART is <u>positive</u>, we have a negative (-) word. (If HEART were negative, we'd have a + word, since 2 -'s make a +.) So look for the <u>opposite</u> of a - word, which is a + (<u>positive word</u>). Now look at the choices. Assign 0 to a neutral word, + to a positive word, and - to a negative word. You can see that Choices D and E are both negative-sounding words because of the prefixes DIS and MIS. Thus we assign a - to these words. (Remember we are looking for a + word). Now look at Choices A and C. These are <u>neutral</u> sounding words, so assign a 0 to them. But look at Choice B, <u>encourage</u>: courage is positive. The prefix <u>en</u> means <u>in</u> or <u>into</u>, so this is also rather positive-sounding. Therefore, we assign a + to the word <u>encourage</u>. It is the only + word, so it must be the correct choice.

Let's look at another example where we can use the +,-, 0 method:

```
UNDERSTATE        (A) embroider
                  (B) initiate
                  (C) distort
                  (D) pacify
                  (E) reiterate
```

UNDER means <u>below</u>, so assign a - to the whole word, being careful to see that STATE is not -. So we are looking for a + word since we want to find an <u>opposite</u>. Choices B and E are neutral, so assign a 0 to them. Choice C is negative, so assign a minus (-) to that word. Now look at Choices A and D. Although PACIFY sounds positive, EMBROIDER sounds much more <u>actively positive</u>, so I would choose Choice A over Choice D. (And I'd be correct).

Many times you may get an antonym question correct by just being able to associate the word with a related word or a word with a similar feel. Here's an example of what I mean:

FIREBRAND   (A) an intellect
                 (B) one who is charitable
                 (C) one who makes peace
                 (D) a philanthropist
                 (E) one who is dishonest

Here you should get the feeling from FIRE in FIREBRAND that FIREBRAND is a very harsh or violent-sounding word. Therefore, an opposite would be some word that would impart a quiet or peaceful feeling. Choice C fits the bill!

Here's another example:

LEVITY   (A) insightfulness
              (B) sincerity
              (C) viciousness
              (D) smoothness
              (E) curiosity

Think of what levity could mean. What other words might contain the root lev? Elevate means to raise up. Levitate means much the same thing. So lev probably has something to do with raising up. How does this help? None of the choices means "putting down." But in using this strategy, you are not looking for literal meanings. You are more concerned with the feel of the words. The feel of the root lev is lightness, airiness. The feel opposite to this is heaviness or seriousness. So Choice B, sincerity, is your best choice.

ANALOGIES

In the Analogies section of the SAT, the questions follow the pattern of this example:

```
WING : BIRD ::        (A)  dog:cat
                      (B)  hair:barber
                      (C)  stripes:tiger
                      (D)  fin:fish
                      (E)  grass:lawn
```

In these questions, a pair of words or phrases written in capitals is followed by five other pairs of words or phrases. The capitalized words are related in some way. You have to find the pair of words in the choices that are related in the same way. In the example, you can see that a WING is what a BIRD uses to move. Among the choices is a pair that expresses a similar relationship: a <u>fin</u> is what a <u>fish</u> uses to move. So Choice D is the best answer.

Sometimes an analogy is read like this: "A wing is to a bird as a <u>what</u> is to a <u>what</u>?" Or, "A wing is to a bird what a fin is to a fish." Reading an analogy this way is not much help in finding an answer. The strategies below will show you better ways.

Make sentences out of the analogy.

The <u>key strategy</u> in working with an analogy is to put the analogy into sentence form. First start with the capitalized words. Make up a sentence that expresses or defines the relationship between them. Here's an example of what I mean:

```
PRACTICE : IMPROVEMENT ::     (A)  work:effort
                             (B)  help:achievement
                             (C)  sanding:smoothness
                             (D)  praise:envy
                             (E)  running:trophies
```

Making a sentence out of the capitalized words, you might say,

PRACTICE will give me IMPROVEMENT.

or

The purpose of PRACTICE is to get IMPROVEMENT.

The second step is to substitute words in the choices for the capitalized words in your sentence. Which substitution makes most sense? In the example above, you should find that the best choice is:

SANDING will give me SMOOTHNESS.

or

The purpose of SANDING is to get SMOOTHNESS.

No other pair of words substitutes as well. So Choice C is correct.

Notice how this strategy lets you zero in on the correct answer without your having to waste time analyzing the relationships between the words in the incorrect choices. The important thing is to start off with a sentence that <u>accurately</u> expresses the relationship between the capitalized words of the question.

STRATEGY
13

Become familiar with some of the principal types of analogy.

There are numerous types or categories of analogies that are used in the SAT. You do not have to learn them, but you should become familiar with some of the most important. Doing this will give you a good feel of what you should expect to find in this section of the SAT, and what you should look for when you construct your Analogy Sentences.

Here is a table containing several types of analogies:

```
Type:        LESSER DEGREE:GREATER DEGREE
Examples:    smile:laugh   breathe:pant   cut:slash
------------------------------------------------------------------
Type:        WORD:SYNONYM (the synonym may be a different part of speech)
Examples:    liar:mendacious   collapse:debacle   liar:prevarication
------------------------------------------------------------------
Type:        CAUSE:EFFECT
Examples:    practice:improvement   punch:pain   bombing:destruction
------------------------------------------------------------------
Type:        PART:WHOLE
Examples:    bird:flock   violinist:orchestra   pitcher:baseball team
------------------------------------------------------------------
Type:        GENERAL:SPECIFIC
Examples:    pain-killer:aspirin   poem:sonnet   vehicle:train
------------------------------------------------------------------
Type:        THING:QUALITY OF THING
Examples:    sandpaper:rough   water:wet   skunk:smell
------------------------------------------------------------------
Type:        OBJECT:USE
Examples:    scissors:cut   car:transportation   heatlamp:warmth
------------------------------------------------------------------
Type:        USER:TOOL
Examples:    sculptor:chisel   photographer:camera   potter:wheel
------------------------------------------------------------------
```

Any of the above types is equally likely to appear on the SAT in reverse order. Thus EFFECT:CAUSE may be used instead of CAUSE:EFFECT, and so on. (Of course, the items in the correct choice will be in the same order as the items in the question. If the order of two items in the question is EFFECT:CAUSE, then the order of items in one possible correct choice would be pain:punch.)

There are many other possible types of analogy in addition to the ones listed above. However, the list should give you a good idea of the variety of relationships that the Analogy section tests for. Look the list over carefully, and make sure you understand each type.

Don't create too simple an analogy.

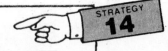

How simple -- or how subtle -- should your analogy sentence be? Here's an example to guide you:

```
HELMET : HEAD ::    (A)  sword:warrior
                    (B)  umbrella:clothing
                    (C)  shoe:stocking
                    (D)  watch:wrist
                    (E)  thimble:finger
```

You might be content to create a sentence like: A HELMET is worn on the HEAD. But the relationship between HELMET and HEAD that it expresses is too simple (a hat is worn on the head, too.) If you created this sentence, you might think that D was the correct answer, since a watch is worn on the wrist.

A sentence that better expresses the relationship between HELMET and HEAD is

A HELMET is put on the HEAD to protect it.

With this sentence as a guide, you can see that the correct answer is E, since a thimble is put on a finger to protect it.

A word of caution: Don't make the connecting words of your sentence too specific, or you will miss the relationship you are looking for. For example, if the capitalized words are WING:BIRD, avoid constructing a sentence like this one:

A WING is what a BIRD uses to fly with.

The word fly is too specific! It describes the specific motion of a bird, not the general idea that a wing moves a bird. If you construct a sentence like the one above, you'll miss the choice fin:fish. (You can't say that a fin is what a fish uses to fly with -- unless you're talking about flying fish.)

STRATEGY 15

Try reversing the order of the words before constructing your sentence.

You may find that in certain cases you can construct a clearer, simpler sentence if you reverse the order of the key words in it. Here's an example:

```
DISEASE : VACCINATION ::        (A)  cavity:dentist
                                (B)  medicine:potion
                                (C)  orchestra:conductor
                                (D)  plant:serum
                                (E)  spoilage:freezing
```

Here you might wish to construct a sentence with the words in reverse order. Your sentence might read:

VACCINATION prevents DISEASE

When you substitute, you must reverse the order of the choices too! Doing this, we can see that <u>freezing</u> prevents <u>spoilage</u>, and Choice E is the best answer.

Don't forget -- if you reverse the order of the capitalized words, you must also reverse the order of the words in the choices!

STRATEGY 16

Pay close attention to grammatical clues.

Very often the two capitalized words in an analogy will be two different grammatical parts of speech. The commonest paring is noun with adjective. Some examples would be: KNOWLEDGE:IGNORANT ; POISON:VENOMOUS ; DAREDEVIL:RECKLESS ; etc. (In all these examples the noun is first and the adjective second, but in the actual SAT the order could be either way.)

Here's the strategy. Whenever you notice a noun-adjective pair, the chances are very high that the two words will be, in effect, either synonyms or antonyms. In the examples above, the first pair of words are antonyms, the last two pairs are synonyms.

This strategy may help you in either of two ways. First, it can give you a hint about how to construct a test sentence of the type described in the last two strategies. Second, it may help you if you don't know the meaning of one of the capitalized words and have to guess. For example:

```
LIAR : MENDACIOUS ::        (A)  disease:carrier
                            (B)  artist:creative
                            (C)  conductor:symphonic
                            (D)  pygmy:undersized
                            (E)  fib:concerned
```

Here we would say that since MENDACIOUS looks like an adjective, it probably describes either what a liar is, or the opposite of what a liar is. (So it probably either means ly-ing or truthful.) Looking over the choices, we find one pair of words that mean the same: pygmy and undersized. Since there are no word pairs that are opposites, the correct choice is probably D.

Beware of superficial relationships.

STRATEGY 17

In almost every analogy question, the test maker designs one or more choices to trap you.

One very common trap consists of a word pair that has the same subject matter as the capitalized words, but has a different relationship. For example:

```
MUSIC : VIOLIN ::   (A)  wood:hammer
                    (B)  furniture:carpentry tools
                    (C)  symphony:piano
                    (D)  society:people
                    (E)  notes:composer
```

In the example, Choices C and E are about music, just as the capitalized words are. You might get fooled into choosing one of these choices if you didn't notice that the relationships between the word pairs in these choices are not the same as the relationship between MUSIC and VIOLIN. (To construct a reversed sentence -- A VIOLIN is a device for making MUSIC. But an orchestra -- not a piano -- is used to play a symphony. And a composer is not a device for making notes.) The correct choice is B: furniture is made with carpentry tools just as MUSIC is made by a VIOLIN.

A second common trap is to insert a pair of words whose relationship is similar in a vague or weak way to that of the capitalized words. For example, let's look once again at this analogy that you worked with earlier:

```
PRACTICE : IMPROVEMENT ::      (A)  work:effort
                               (B)  help:achievement
                               (C)  sanding:smoothness
                               (D)  praise:envy
                               (E)  running:trophies
```

All the choices except C, the correct answer, are traps of this kind! B and E are big traps. Help sometimes results in achievement, and running may lead to a trophy (if you win). But a closer look should show you that the relationships are much fuzzier than the clear relationships between PRACTICE and IMPROVEMENT on the one hand and sanding and smoothness on the other.

Work and effort look related (although backwards) -- but a more careful look shows you that it's not true that effort leads to work as PRACTICE leads to IMPROVEMENT. And although praise may cause envy, it causes envy in others, and it is not usually designed for the purpose of causing envy.

Be careful of these traps. The best way to avoid them is to make a well-constructed key sentence using the capitalized words. If your sentence does a good job of showing the true relationship between the capitalized words, the traps are less likely to catch you.

SENTENCE COMPLETION

The questions in the Sentence Completion section begin with a sentence that has one or two words missing. You have to find the missing words or words. Here's a very simple example:

> You may think Bill is tall, but his brother is even _____.
>
> (A) younger
> (B) taller
> (C) older
> (D) wiser
> (E) happier

The best word to fill in the blank is Choice B, taller.

STRATEGY 18

Watch for Key Words in the sentence.

As you can see from the example above, the sentence is constructed with enough clues for you to find the missing words. You have to watch for key words that link the sentence together. Or watch for key words that give you the tone of the sentence. The important linkage words are words like but, while, if, and, because, although, since, by contrast to, nevertheless, etc. Key words like powerful, only, long range, describe the extent to which something is happening, and are also important.

STRATEGY 19

Try to complete the sentence before you look at the choices.

You will often find that the quickest, easiest way of finding the missing word or words is to try and complete the sentence by yourself, without looking at the choices at all.

Then, after you have come up with your own word or words to complete the sentence, you can look among the choices. Chances are good that you will find your word or another one with a meaning close to it. For example:

Although the senator was admired personally, his ideas and policies were not _____.

    (A) initiated   (B) well founded
    (C) supported   (D) contrived
          (E) interesting

The key word although gives it away. It contrasts one part of the sentence with the other. The word although tells us that in one case the senator was liked, but in another case something negative is happening to his ideas and policies. So, even without looking at the choices, we can see that the senator's ideas were not well accepted, supported, etc. We can see then that Choice C fits the bill without analyzing the other choices. Note that in this example, you could have tried to fit all the choices (A), (B), etc. into the sentence, but in a case like this it is easier and more efficient to complete the sentence by yourself, supported by understanding the gist of the sentence and how the word although contrasts the two parts of the sentence.

Just in case some of you wonder why Choice B is not correct: As the senator was admired, something has to be done to the senator. So a choice like accepted, supported, etc. is active; this is done to the senator. And so, Choice C fits the bill. But a choice like well founded is part of the senator's ideas, and not something done actively to the senator, as acceptance or support.

Let's try a sentence completion question involving <u>two</u> missing words:

> Science is forever trying to understand the _____ aspects of the universe; one day mankind will possibly understand the _____ structure of nature.
>
> (A) important...simulated
> (B) grandiose...simple
> (C) philosophical...poetic
> (D) direct...complete
> (E) fundamental...basic

Here there must be a link between the two parts. We should realize that the adjective modifying the word <u>aspects</u> must be related to the adjective modifying the word <u>structure</u>. Very likely the words will mean the same thing. So you can see that Choice E, <u>fundamental...basic</u> fits the bill.

These two - missing - word sentence completions are somewhat more difficult than the one-word missing sentence completions, but if you can figure out the linkage of the parts in the sentence and how the missing words supply the linkage, you will make the question fairly easy.

Note that in the above example, you could have tried substituting all the choices in the sentence. You would then see that Choice A does not make too much sense, then you would see that Choice B is almost contradictory with words like <u>grandiose</u> and <u>simple</u>. You could use this method substituting the rest of the choice sets. But, note that if you really understood the gist of the sentence and that you were looking for words of similar meaning, you could almost zero in on Choice E as being the correct one. And, although you can always substitute all the choices to test them for correctness, the best way to answer these sentence completion questions is to try to zero in on the correct choice without having to substitute the rest of the incorrect choices. Be cautious, though - in <u>some</u> cases you may not be astute enough to find a clever linkage in the sentence and in that case it would be better for you to substitute in all the choices. In that case, I would <u>start with Choice E and work backwards</u> substituting Choice D next, then Choice C, etc., in that order. Many times, when the test taker has to substitute all the choices, the test maker will make sure that the correct answer is either Choice D or E, the correct answer being at the far end of the choices. This insures that if the test taker makes a mistake in the first few choices and gets one of the first choices as an answer, he/she will be justifiably penalized for the wrong answer.

STRATEGY
20

Look for negative-positive contrasts.

Sometimes it is possible to zero in immediately on the correct choice by noting that one part of the sentence has a positive (or negative) feeling whereas the other part of the sentence has a negative (or positive) feeling. So for one blank you would choose a positive (or negative) word and for the other blank you would choose a word that has an opposite feeling (a negative or positive) word. Here's a typical SAT example:

> When Mr. Simmons _____ a thought, he discounts it cleverly, but when anything appeals to him, he is able to be _____ enough.
>
> (A) discovers...fearful
> (B) thinks of...irresponsible
> (C) analyzes...distrustful
> (D) is uncomfortable with...responsive
> (E) is afraid of...hostile

The key words are discounts and but. The word but contrasts an opposite feeling to the one brought out in the first part of the sentence. The word discounts has a negative feeling, so the word in the first blank probably has a negative feeling. Because the word but in the second part of the sentence contrasts with the first part, and because of the positive nature of the word appeals, the second blank must require a positive-sounding word. Note that of all the choices, the only choice that describes a negative word for the first blank and a positive word for the second blank is Choice D. And so, Choice D is correct.

Here's another example illustrating again the above point:

She is so far from achieving a true _____ of human relations that she has _____ almost completely unto herself.
(A) perspective...developed
(B) understanding...withdrawn
(C) animosity...retreated
(D) void...managed
(E) value...transformed

In the first part of the sentence, the words true and human relations suggest a positive feeling and the words so far from and that indicate a negative feeling in the second part of the sentence. Also the words almost completely unto herself suggest a negative feeling. Thus the first blank must be positive and the second blank must be negative. The only choice that fits the bill is Choice B. Note that in Choice A the word developed has positive or neutral connotations, and in Choice E the word transformed is neutral. Thus Choices A and E are incorrect.

Work "backwards" from the part of the sentence without the blank.

You will often be able to zero in on the missing word in a sentence by carefully considering the part of the sentence <u>without</u> the blank. For example:

> Insight is so _____ in problem-solving that we seem to take it for granted.
>
> (A) extraordinary
> (B) theoretical
> (C) partial
> (D) important
> (E) common

The part of the sentence without the blank is <u>we seem to take it for granted</u>, and there are no "negative" linking key words like <u>but</u> or <u>although</u>. What is something that we would take for granted? Something ordinary, everyday, expected. Choice E, <u>common</u>, fits the bill perfectly.

A negative key linking word in this sentence would signal you to look for the <u>opposite</u> of the part of the sentence without the blank. For example, suppose the sentence had been this one:

> Although common sense is actually _____, we nevertheless take it for granted.

Here the key words <u>although</u> and <u>nevertheless</u> tell you to look for the opposite of something you would <u>take for granted</u>. The best word would be something like <u>rare</u>, <u>unusual</u>, or <u>uncommon</u>.

Remember -- when you work backward from the part of the sentence without the blank, be sure to check for key linking words that shows you how it relates to the part with the blank.

**Don't panic if you see difficult words in the choices.
Sometimes the easier words have the answer.**

Sometimes you may understand the meaning of every word in the sentence, but not in the choices. Should you give up? Should you guess? Here's an example:

Let us not _____ the man for his action; he could not have been aware of the _____ of his crime.

(A) criticize...animosity
(B) excommunicate...nature
(C) promulgate...timeliness
(D) condemn...gravity
(E) belittle...legality

Here you may not know what the words promulgate, excommunicate or animosity mean. And you may not want to spend time looking at the other two choice sets. In that case you would be wise to guess and go on to the next question on the test. However, you may try to quickly see the gist of the sentence. Note that the sentence implies that we are not going to do something as the person was not aware of the extent of the crime. Doesn't it look like Choice D is correct? If you didn't know the meaning of gravity, just think of gravity on the earth. Gravity makes things heavy, so you'd be on safe ground assuming that the word gravity meant something that is heavy. Now the sentence makes sense if we say...Let us not CONDEMN the man for his action; he could not have been aware of the GRAVITY of his crime.

READING COMPREHENSION

The Reading Comprehension sections of the SAT contain passages of about 100 to 500 words in length. After each passage there is a set of 2 to 5 questions. (Longer passages have 4-5 questions, shorter passages have 2-3 questions.)

STRATEGY
23

Become familiar with the main categories of reading questions.

It will be very useful for you to become familiar with the principal types of questions that are asked after each reading selection. By becoming familiar with these types, you will get a feel for what you should concentrate on in your reading of the passage, and you will in addition be prepared for the many of the actual questions that follow the passage. The principal types are --

1. Questions based on the passage as a whole.
2. Questions based on one or more specific sections of the passage.
3. Questions based on particular words, phrases, or sentences.

The lists below contain the typical recurring question types found in each main category, as derived from analysis of actual SAT's. Each listed question type is followed by one or more examples of the kind of wording that the SAT uses in its actual questions.

. . . .

Questions based on the passage as a whole

Question Type	Examples of SAT Wording
1. MAIN POINT - What is the passage trying to tell you?	The passage is mainly concerned with ...

Question Type	Examples of SAT Wording
2. PRIMARY PURPOSE OF AUTHOR – What does the author want to tell you?	The author's primary purpose in the passage is to ...
3. MOOD OR ATTITUDE OF AUTHOR – What is the tone or attitude of the author?	On the basis of the passage, the author's attitude toward Mrs. Alden can most accurately be termed as one of ...
4. ASSUMPTIONS MADE BY AUTHOR – What assumptions are made by the author but not directly stated in the passage?	Which of the following is an assumption made by the author?
5. APPLICATIONS OF MAIN IDEAS – How can you extend the main ideas of the passage?	The author provides information that would answer all of the following questions EXCEPT... According to the author, the effort of taking a nation-wide vote on the proposed program would be ...
6. IMPLICATIONS OF PASSAGE OR OF THE AUTHOR – What does the author or the passage imply?	The author implies that a work of art is properly judged on the basis of its ...
7. SUMMARY OF PASSAGE – In a few words how would you describe the passage? What title would you give the passage?	Which of the following titles best summarizes the content of the passage? Which of the following would be the most appropriate title for the passage?
8. CONTENT OF THE PASSAGE – What is the passage really about?	Which of the following describes the content of the passage?
9. INFERENCES – What can you infer from the passage as a whole?	It can be inferred from the passage that the ...
10. STATEMENTS THAT THE AUTHOR WOULD BE IN AGREEMENT WITH – What could you say that the author would agree with, knowing the way he wrote the passage?	With which of the following statements regarding ragtime would the author probably agree?

Questions based on one or more specific sections of the passage

Question Type	Examples of SAT Wording
1. INFERENCES - What can you infer from specific sections in the passage?	It can be inferred that the ancients' atomic theory was primarily based on ...
2. APPLICATIONS - How can you apply information in specific sections of the passage to other areas?	The author provides information that answers which of the following questions?
3. WHAT PRECEDES PASSAGE OR COMES AFTER PASSAGE - What do you think was written right before the passage or right after the passage?	It can be inferred that in the paragraphs immediately preceding the passage, the author discussed ...
4. STATED IDEAS - Can you find in the passage a specific reference to a stated idea?	According to the passage, blacks were denied entrance into anti-slavery societies because ...
5. IMPLICATIONS - What is implied by a section in the passage?	The author implies that many American's devotion to the ideal of brotherhood of man is ... In describing American attitudes about the land (lines 7-8), the author implies that ...
6. TONE OR MOOD - What is the tone or mood of a section in the passage?	At the conclusion of the passage, the author's tone is one of ...

....

Questions based on particular words, phrases, or sentences

Question Type	Examples of SAT Wording
1. REASON FOR USE - Why are certain words or phrases or sentences mentioned or used in the passage?	The author mentions Newton's Principia in order to ...

Question Type	Examples of SAT Wording
2. MEANING OF A WORD OR PHRASE - What is the meaning of a certain word, phrase, or sentence in the passage?	The enemy referred to in the last sentence is probably ... According to the author, the words in the Declaration of Independence, "all men are created equal," were meant to represent ... By "this skepticism" (line 35), the author means ...

STRATEGY 24

Read the passage and anticipate the questions that might be asked about it.

The key approach for doing well on answering reading comprehension questions is getting involved and interested in the passage before you read the questions. While you read the passage, try to figure out the motive of the person that wrote the passage. Why is he or she saying what is in the passage? Do you agree or disagree with what is being said? Are you angry at what is being stated? You will find that if you get interested and involved in reading the passage, you will be able to anticipate many of the test questions.

And this brings me to a question many test-takers ask: "Should I look at the questions before reading the passage?" The answer I usually give students is that you can use one of two methods: You can look at the questions (not the choices!) first. But if you do, you may spend time that you could have used reading the passage. On the other hand, if you can get involved with the passage, you will, in fact, anticipate many of the questions that follow the passage. And in that case, there would be no point in wasting any time in looking at the questions, first. In your practice you may want to try it both ways and see which way proves best for you.

To give you an idea of what I mean, look over the following passage. When you are done, I'll show you how you might read it so as to get involved with the passage and with the author's intent.

We should also know that "greed" has little to do with the environmental crisis. The two main causes are population pressures, especially the pressures of large metropolitan populations, and the desire - a highly commmendable one - to bring a decent living at the lowest possible cost to the largest possible number of people.

The environmental crisis is the result of success - success in cutting down the mortality of infants (which has given us the population explosion), success in raising farm output sufficiently to prevent mass famine (which has given us contamination by pesticides and chemical fertilizers), success in getting the people out of the tenements of the 19th-century cities and into the greenery and privacy of the single-family home in the suburbs (which has given us urban sprawl and traffic jams). The environmental crisis, in other words, is largely the result of doing too much of the right sort of thing.

To overcome the problems that success always creates, one must build on it. But where to start? Cleaning up the environment requires determined, sustained effort with clear targets and deadlines. It requires, above all, concentration of effort. Up to now we have tried to do a little bit of everything - and tried to do it in the headlines - when what we ought to do first is draw up a list of priorities.

Now I'll go over the passage with you, showing you what might go through your mind as you read. This will let you see how to get involved with the passage, and how this involvement facilitates answering the questions that follow the passage. In many cases, you'll actually be able to anticipate the questions. Of course, when you are preparing for the SAT, you'll have to develop this skill so that you do it rapidly and almost automatically.

Let's look at the first sentence:

We should also know that "greed" has little to do with the environmental crisis.

Immediately you should say to yourself, "So something else must be involved with the environmental crisis." Read on:

The two main causes are population pressures, especially the pressures of large metropolitan populations, and the desire - a highly commendable one - to bring a decent living at the lowest possible cost to the largest possible number of people.

Now you can say to yourself, "Oh, so population pressures and the desire to help out the people in the community caused the environmental crisis." You should also get a feeling that the author is not really against these causes of the environmental crisis, and that he or she believes that the crisis is in part a side effect of worthwhile efforts and enterprises. Read on:

The environmental crisis is the result of success - success in cutting down the mortality of infants (which has given us the population explosion), success in raising farm output sufficiently to prevent mass famine (which has given us contamination by pesticides and chemical fertilizers), success in getting the people out of the tenements of the 19th-century city and into the greenery and privacy of the single-family home in the suburbs (which has given us urban sprawl and traffic jams).

Now you should say to yourself, "It seems that for every positive thing that the author mentions, there is a negative occurence which leads to the environmental crisis."

Now read the last sentence of this paragraph:

The environmental crisis, in other words, is largely the result of doing too much of the right sort of thing.

Now you can say to yourself, "Gee, we wanted to do the right thing, but we created something bad. It looks like you can't have your cake and eat it, too!"

Now you should anticipate that in the next and final paragraph, the author will discuss what may be done to reduce the bad effects which come from the good. Look at the first sentence of the third paragraph:

To overcome the problem that success always creates, one must build on it.

Now you can say to yourself, "Well, how?" In fact, in the next sentence the author asks the very question you just asked: But where to start? Read on to find out the author's answer:

Cleaning up the environment requires determined, sustained effort with clear targets and deadlines. It requires, above all, concentration and effort.

So now you can say to yourself, "Oh so that's what we need – definite goals, deadlines for reaching those goals, and genuine effort to achieve the goals."

The author then discusses what you may have already thought about:

Up to now we have tried to do a little bit of everything -

What the author is saying (and you should realize this) is that up to now, we haven't concentrated on one particular problem at a time. We used "buckshots instead of bullets." Read on:

- and tried to do it in the headlines - when what we ought to do first is to draw up a list of priorities.

So you can now see that, in the author's opinion, making a list of priorities and working on them one at a time, with a target in mind, may get us out of the environmental crisis and still preserve our quality of life.

Before we start to answer the questions, let me just tell you the best and most effective way of answering passage questions. You should read the question and proceed to look at the choices in the order of Choice A, Choice B, etc. If a choice (such as Choice A) doesn't give you the definite feeling that it is correct, don't try to analyze it further. Go on to Choice B. Again, if that choice (Choice B) doesn't make you feel that it's the right one, and you really have to think carefully about the choice, go on to Choice C. The first choice that you have a definite feeling of being correct (let's say it's Choice C), is the one you should mark on your answer sheet. Don't bother going on to the rest of the choices. In other words, stop at the choice that you feel is obviously the right one.

Suppose you have gone through all the five choices, and you don't know which one is correct, or you don't see any one that stands out as obviously being correct. Then quickly guess, and go on to the next question. You can go back after you have answered the other questions relating to the passage. But remember, when you go back to the questions you weren't sure of, don't spend too much time on them. Try to forge ahead on the test.

Let's proceed to answer the questions now.

Look at the first question:

1. This passage assumes the desirability of
    (A) using atomic energy to conserve fuel
    (B) living in comfortable family lifestyles
    (C) settling disputes peacefully
    (D) combating cancer and heart disease with energetic research
    (E) having greater government involvement in people's daily lives

Look at Choice A. That doesn't seem correct. Now look at Choice B. Do you remember that the author claimed that the environmental crisis is the result of the successful attempt to get people out of their tenements into a better environment? We can only feel that the author assumes this desirability of living in comfortable family lifestyles (Choice B) since the author uses the word success in describing the transition from living in tenements to living in single-family homes. Therefore Choice B is correct. You don't need to analyze or even consider the other choices, since we have zeroed in on Choice B.

Let's look at Question 2:

2. According to this passage, one early step in any effort
    to improve the environment would be to
    (A) return to the exclusive use of natural fertilizers
    (B) put a high tax on profiteering industries
    (C) ban the use of automobiles in the cities
    (D) study successful efforts in other countries
    (E) set up a timetable for corrective actions

Again let's go through the choices in the order Choice A,
Choice B, etc. until we come up with the right choice. Choices
A, B, C and D seem unlikely to be correct, but we may want to
go back to Choices C and D. Now look at Choice E. We remember
that the author said that we should get "clear targets and
deadlines" to improve the environment. That looks pretty much
as if Choice E is correct.

Let's look at Question 3:

3. The passage indicates that the conditions that led to
    overcrowded roads also brought about
    (A) more attractive living conditions for many people
    (B) a healthier younger generation
    (C) greater occupational opportunities
    (D) the population explosion
    (E) greater concentration of population pressures

Here we would want to go back to the part where over-
crowded roads was discussed in the passage. This is where
(2nd paragraph) the author says that "urban sprawl and traffic
jams" are one result of success in getting people out of
tenements to single-family homes. So you can see that Choice A
is correct. Again, no need to consider other choices, since
you should be fairly comfortable with Choice A.

Let's look at Question 4:

4. It could logically be assumed that the author of this
    passage would support legislation to
    (A) ban the use of all pesticides
    (B) prevent the use of automobiles in the cities
    (C) build additional conventional power plants
        immediately
    (D) organize an agency to coordinate efforts to cope
        with environmental problems
    (E) restrict the press coverage of protest led by
        environmental groups

This is the type of question which asks you to understand what the author would feel about something else, when
you already know something about the author's sentiments on
one particular subject.

Choices A, B, and C do not seem correct. But look at
Choice D. The author said that the way to get out of the
energy crisis is to set targets and deadlines in order to
cope with specific problems. The author would therefore
probably organize an agency to do this. Choice D is correct.

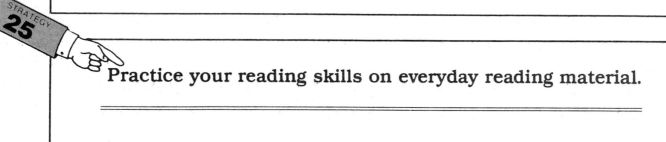

Practice your reading skills on everyday reading material.

You do not have much opportunity to practice SAT math
skills in everyday life. But you have every opportunity in
the world to sharpen your reading comprehension skills.

Read selections form any of the following sources:

Newspaper stories   Science fact magazines
Newspaper editorials   Encyclopedia articles
Newspaper political columns   Nonfiction books
News magazines (particular-   General interest magazines
  ly columns and essays)   like Reader's Digest

When you read any selection, read it in units of 3 to
6 paragraphs -- units about the length of an actual SAT selection. As you read it, keep in mind the question types
listed in the first strategy of this section. When you are
done, go to the list of question types and use them as a
guide to make up your own questions for the selection, as
if you were a test maker for the SAT. Then answer your own
questions. The practice this will give you will help enor-
mously when you take the SAT. And it will make you a better
reader as well.

MATH
STRATEGIES

MATH PREP

This chapter contains material specifically designed to pre-pare you for the detailed math strategies that follow. The chapter is organized with three sections:

Test Yourself enables you to find out quickly where you need to brush up on your math.

Correct Yourself gives you the answers to the test questions -- plus instructions on each test problem so that you can tutor yourself on any problem area.

Arm Yourself contains instructional summaries of the principal math formulas and equivalencies that you need to know to use the math strategies effectively.

Test Yourself

Spend 30 minutes or less taking the test on the fol-lowing pages. The questions on this test are much easier than the ones on the actual SAT. Nevertheless, do not skip over this section! The test is a review and summary of the principal mathematical operations that the SAT test makers use as the basis for constructing their test questions! So this entire section is actually a giant basic strategy. You must know all this material to perform successfully on the SAT and to understand -- and use -- the specific math strategies outlined in the rest of this book.

When you have finished the test, go on to the next section, Correct Yourself. There you will find the answers to the Test Yourself questions, plus additional instruction.

Remember: you must be able to get every question correct, and understand why, before you go on with the rest of the book.

....

These questions test your ability and background in working with FACTORS.

1. $(x + 5)(x - 4) =$

_____

2. $(x-y)^2 =$

_____

3. $-(x - y) =$

_____

4.   Factor: $a^2 - b^2$

_____

These questions test your ability and background in working with EXPONENTS.

5. $10^4 =$

_____

6. $x^3 \times x^8 =$

_____

7. $(xy)^5 =$

_____

8. $a^{-4} \times a^{+5} =$

_____

9.   What is x^{-4} written with no negative signs?

10. If $x^2 = 4$, what is x?

_____

11. Find: $2^2 + 4^2$

_____

These questions test your ability and background in working with PERCENTS.

12. 22% of 100 =

_____

13. What is 8% of 4?

_____

14. What percent of 7 is 14?

_____

These questions test your ability and background in working with EQUATIONS.

15. What is y in terms of x given
    y - x = 5?

_____

16. Find the value of x and y:
    x + 2y = 3; x - 2y = 1

_____

These questions test your ability and background in working with ANGLES.

17.

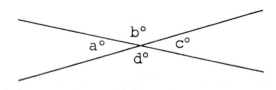

In the diagram above, what is the value of
(1) a + b (2) a - c (3) a + b + c + d (4) b - d?

(1) _____   (3) _____

(2) _____   (4) _____

18. What is the value of a + b + c in the diagram below?

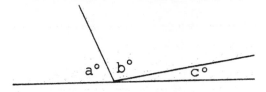

These questions test your ability and background in working with <u>TRIANGLES</u>

19. In the diagram below, is a + b greater than c?

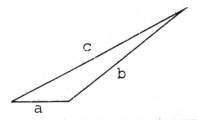

20. In the diagram below, what is the value of x?

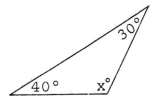

21. In the diagram below, what is y?

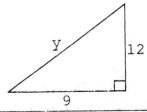

22. In the diagram below, what is a?

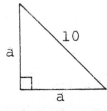

23. What is the area of the triangle below?

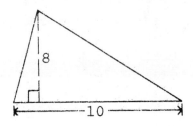

These questions test your ability and background in working with <u>CIRCLES</u>.

24. Find the area and the circumference of the circle:

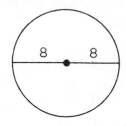

area =

circumference =

_____

25. If AB is a diameter of the circle, what is y?

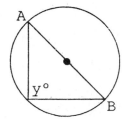

_____

This question tests your ability and background in working with <u>PARALLEL LINES</u>.

26. In the diagram below where l_1 and l_2 are parallel, what is the value of a, b, c, d, and e?

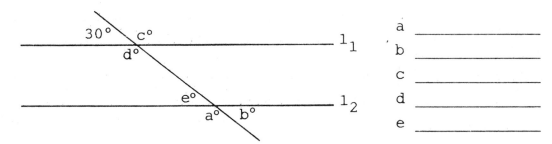

a _____

b _____

c _____

d _____

e _____

_____

This question tests your ability and background in working with <u>NUMBER LINES</u>.

27. Use the signs $>$ (greater than), $<$ (less than), or = (equal) to determine the relative values of a and b:

a _____ -2

a _____ -1

b _____ 2

b _____ 1

This question tests your ability and background in working with COORDINATES.

28. From the diagram below, determine which variables (a, b, c, d) are positive or negative:

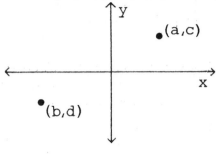

a (positive or negative?) _____

b (positive of negative?) _____

c (positive or negative?) _____

d (positive or negative?) _____

These questions test your ability and background in working with INEQUALITIES.

29. If $a > b$, is $3a > 3b$?

30. If $a + b > c$, is $a > c - b$?

31. If $-3 < p < +3$, is $+3 > -p > -3$?

32. If $a < b$, is $na < nb$?

These questions test your ability and background in working with AVERAGES.

33. What is the average score in a class of 3 students whose scores are 45, 60, and 90 on an exam?

34. What is the average rate of speed of a bicycle traveling 30 miles in 3 hours?

Correct Yourself

EXPLANATORY ANSWERS WITH SHORTCUTS AND STRATEGIES
AND GENERAL MATH REVIEW

FACTORS

1. $(x + 5)(x - 4) = x^2 + 5x - 4x - 20$

    $= \underline{x^2 + x - 20}$

Multiply <u>each</u> quantity in the first factor with <u>each</u> quantity in the second factor. That is,

Multiply x by x to get x^2

Multiply 5 by x to get 5x

Multiply x by -4 to get -4x

Multiply 5 by -4 to get -20

Then add: $x^2 + 5x - 4x - 20 = x^2 + x - 20$

In general $(x + y)(s + t) = xs + ys + xt + yt$

2. Memorize (after working out to convince yourself):

    $(x-y)^2 = \underline{x^2 - 2xy + y^2}$ $(x+y)^2 = x^2 + 2xy + y^2$

3. Memorize (after working out to convince yourself):

    $-(x-y) = \underline{-x + y}$ $x(y+z) = xy + xz$

    $-(x+y) = -x-y$ $x(y-z) = xy - xz$

4. Memorize (after working out to convince yourself):

    $a^2 - b^2 = \underline{(a + b)(a - b)}$

EXPONENTS

5. $10^4 = \underline{1\ 0\ 0\ 0\ 0}$ $10^5 = 1\ 0\ 0\ 0\ 0\ 0$

                  4 zeros   5 zeros

---

6. $x^3 \times x^8 = \underline{x^{11}}$

In general, for any a,b, and x: $x^a \times x^b = x^{a+b}$
(To multiply, add exponents.)

---

7. $(xy)^5 = \underline{x^5 y^5}$

In general, for any n,x, and y: $(xy)^n = x^n y^n$

---

8. $a^{-4} \times a^{+5} = a^{(-4+5)} = a^{+1} = \underline{a}$

In general for any n,m and a:

$$a^{-n} \times a^{+m} = a^{m-n} \;;\; \frac{a^m}{a^n} = a^{m-n}$$

---

9. $x^{-4} = \dfrac{1}{x^4}\;;$

Don't be afraid of negative exponents. In general for any n,

$$x^{-n} = \frac{1}{x^n}$$

---

10.   If $x^2 = 4$, $x = \pm\sqrt{4} = \pm 2$ (Read as "plus or minus two.")

If $x^2 = n$, then $x = \pm\sqrt{n}$ Don't forget the $\pm$ sign!

---

11. $2^2 + 4^2 = 2 \times 2 + 4 \times 4 = 4 + 16 = \underline{20}$

$2^2 = 2 \times 2$; $2^3 = 2 \times 2 \times 2$, etc. $n^4 = n \times n \times n \times n$ (four times)

PERCENTS

12.   22% of 100 = $\frac{22}{100}$ X 100 = $\underline{22}$

RULE:

> of becomes X
> % becomes $\frac{1}{100}$

So, we get   22%   of   100   =

22 ($\frac{1}{100}$) X 100 = $\frac{22}{100}$ X ~~100~~ = 22

---

13.   What is 8% of 4?   Remember to <u>translate</u>:

> <u>What</u> becomes   x (variable x or unknown x)
>
> % becomes $\frac{1}{100}$
>
> <u>is</u> becomes   =   (equals)
>
> <u>of</u> becomes X   (times)

So, What   is   8 %   of   4

x   =   8($\frac{1}{100}$) X 4

$$x = \frac{8}{100} \text{ X } 4 = \frac{32}{100} \text{ or } .32$$

(You could reduce the fraction further, if you wished, to 8/25.)

---

14.   What percent of 7 is 14?

(x)   ($\frac{1}{100}$) X 7 = 14

$$\frac{x}{100} \text{ X } 7 = 14; \quad \frac{x}{100} = 2; \quad x = \underline{200\%}$$

15. If $y - x = 5$ and we want to solve for y alone, let's <u>add</u> x to both sides of the equation:

$$y - x + x = 5 + x$$
$$y = \underline{5 + x}$$

If we had to find what x was in terms of y, we would still add x to both sides:

$$y - x + x = 5 + x$$
$$y = 5 + x$$

Then we would subtract 5 from both sides:

$$y - 5 = 5 + x - 5$$
$$y - 5 = x$$

16. What is the value of x and y if

$$x + 2y = 3$$
$$x - 2y = 1$$

Let's add both equations:

$$x + 2y = 3$$
$$\underline{+ \quad x - 2y = 1}$$

Adding left sides we get:

$$x + x + 2y - 2y = 2x$$

Adding right sides we get:

$$3 + 1 = 4$$

Now we equate left and right sides:

$$2x = 4; \quad \underline{x = 2.}$$

Now take the value x=2, and put this value <u>back</u> into any one of the equations. Let's work with $x + 2y = 3$. If $x = 2$, then we get

$$2 + 2y = 3$$
$$2y = 3 - 2$$
$$2y = 1$$
$$\underline{y = \tfrac{1}{2}}$$

17.

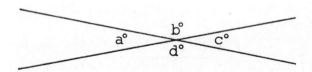

Vertical angles are equal, so a = c, and b = d.

a and b are supplementary angles. So are c and d,
a and d, and c and b. So we get

$$a = c, \quad b = d$$

$$a + b = 180; \quad c + d = 180; \quad a + d = 180; \quad c + b = 180$$

Thus:

(1) $a + b = \underline{180}°$

(2) $a - c = \underline{0}°$ (since a = c)

(3) $a + b + c + d = 180 + 180 = \underline{360}°$

(4) $b - d = \underline{0}°$ (since b = d)

18.

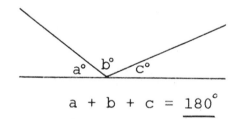

$$a + b + c = \underline{180}°$$

TRIANGLES

19. For any triangle,

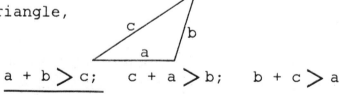

$$\underline{a + b > c}; \quad c + a > b; \quad b + c > a$$

Look at the following
triangle:

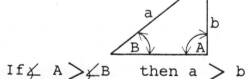

If $\angle A > \angle B$ then a > b

62

20.

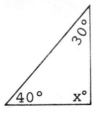

The sum of the interior angles in a triangle = 180°
So,

$$30 + 40 + x = 180°$$
$$70 + x = 180$$
$$x = 180 - 70 = \underline{110°}$$

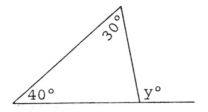

Another useful thing for you to know is that an exterior angle (like y° above) is equal to the sum of the remote interior angles (that is, in the above diagram, y = 30 + 40).

Suppose we have the
following triangle:

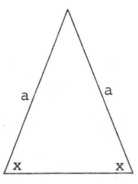

If sides are equal, base angles are equal.

21.

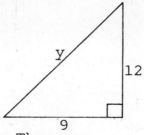

Pythagorean Theorem:

for a right triangle (one angle = 90°)

$$9^2 + 12^2 = y^2$$

$$81 + 144 = y^2$$

$$225 = y^2$$

$$\sqrt{225} = y$$

$$\underline{15} = y$$

In general:

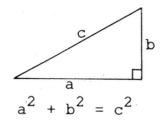

$$a^2 + b^2 = c^2$$

Memorize these right triangles:

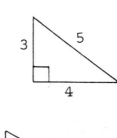

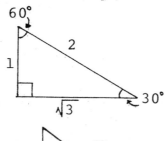

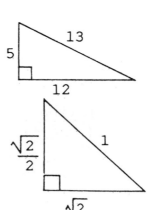

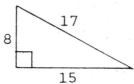

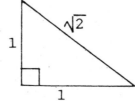

Note that you may multiply each side of the above triangles by a <u>constant</u>:

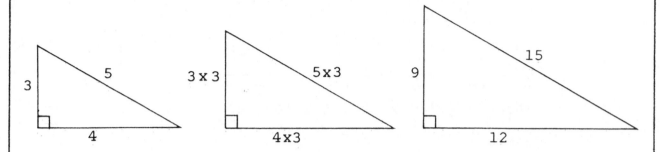

The reason why it is important to be familiar with these right triangles (9,12,15; 3,4,5, etc.) is because of the following. You may be given a right triangle with sides, for example, of 9 and 12. And you may have to find what the third side is. Well, if you know there's a right triangle that has sides 9,12, and 15, you will immediately realize that the third side of a right triangle of sides 9 and 12 is 15. And so you don't have to do any calculation.

22.

$$a^2 + a^2 = 10^2$$

$$2a^2 = 10^2$$

$$a^2 = 100/2$$

$$a^2 = 50$$

$$a = \sqrt{50} = \sqrt{25 \times 2} = \underline{5\sqrt{2}}$$

or look at Triangle (5) in the previous example:

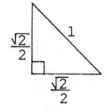

Multiply each side by 10:

So we get a = $5\sqrt{2}$.

65

23.

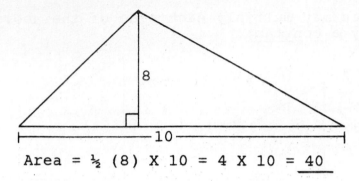

Area = ½ (8) X 10 = 4 X 10 = <u>40</u>

In general:

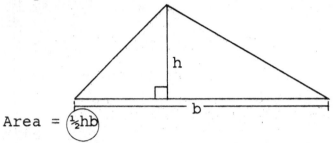

Area = (½hb)

or if we have:

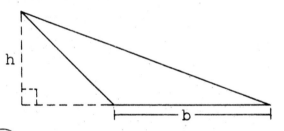

Area is still (½hb)

Area of rectangle:

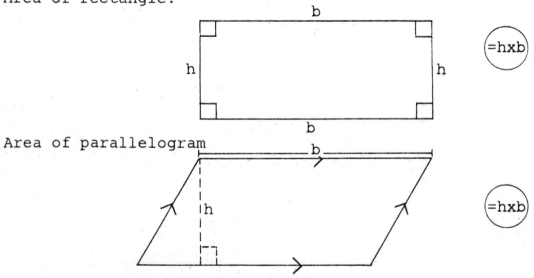

(=hxb)

Area of parallelogram

(=hxb)

24.

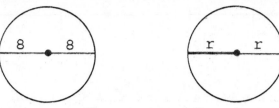

Area $= \pi r^2 = \pi (8)^2 = \underline{64 \pi}$

Circumference $= 2 \pi r = 2 \pi (8) = \underline{16 \pi}$

---

25. If AB is diameter of circle, then arc AB is 180°.

$y°$ is measured by ½ arc so $y = ½(180) = \underline{90}°$.

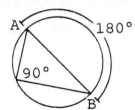

In general: An inscribed angle is measured by
½ the arc it cuts.

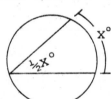

PARALLEL LINES

26.

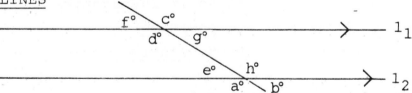

$f + d = 180$; $f + c = 180$; $e + d = 180$; $a + e = 180$;

$a + b = 180$, $e = g$, $d = h$, $e = b$, $f = g$, $f = e$, $c = h$

So if we have $f = 30$, then $d = 150$ and $e = 30$

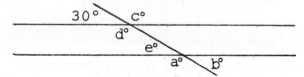

$a = d = \underline{150}$, $b = e = \underline{30}$, $c = d = \underline{150}$, $d = \underline{150}$, $e = \underline{30}$

27.

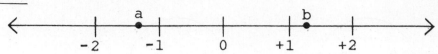

a is between -1 and -2 so -2 $<$ a $<$ -1 and so

a $<$ -1,   a $>$ -2

b is between +1 and +2 so, 1 $<$ b $<$ 2, and so

b $<$ 2, and b $>$ 1

If you have trouble remembering the difference between $>$ and $<$, try remembering that the "open mouth" of the symbol is always on the side of the greater quantity. So a $>$ b means that <u>a</u> is greater; a $<$ b means that <u>b</u> is greater (or a is less)

COORDINATES

28.

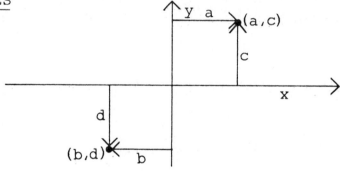

a is to the <u>right</u> so it is <u>positive</u>

b is to the <u>left</u> so it is <u>negative</u>

c is <u>up</u> so it is <u>positive</u>

d is <u>down</u> so it is <u>negative</u>

In general:

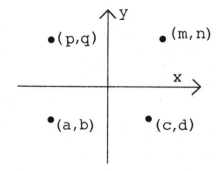

m $>$ 0; n $>$ 0; p $<$ 0; q $>$ 0; a $<$ 0;
b $<$ 0; c $>$ 0; d $<$ 0

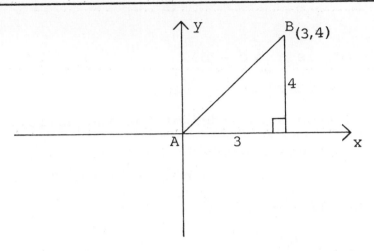

From the above the length AB = $\sqrt{3^2 + 4^2} = \sqrt{5^2} = 5$

INEQUALITIES

29. If $a > b$, is $3a > 3b$?

We work with <u>inequalities</u> almost the same way that we work with <u>equalities</u>. For example:

$$3 = 3$$

Multiply both sides by 2:

We get: 2 X 3 = 2 X 3

So suppose we have

$$3 > 2$$

We can multiply (or divide) both sides of the inequality by the same positive number and still get the same inequality sign. Let's multiply both sides of the inequality $3 > 2$ by 5.

We get: 5 X 3 $>$ 5 X 2

So, as an example, if $a > b$,   then <u>$3a > 3b$</u>.

Note that if we multiply an inequality by a - (minus) sign we must <u>reverse</u> the order of the inequality.

That is, if $a > b$ and we multiply by -1, we get

$$-a < -b$$

30. If $a + b > c$, is $a > c - b$?

Work as if we have an $=$ sign:

Subtract b from both sides of the inequality:

$$a + b - b > c - b$$
$$a > c - b$$

In general, if $a + b > c$

then, $a + b - d > c - d$

Also if $a > b$ then

$$a - m > b - m$$

or if $a > b$

$$a + m > b + m$$

That is, you can also add a number to both sides of an inequality and still get the same relationship of the inequality.

---

31. If $-3 < p < +3$ is $3 > -p > -3$?

Multiply by (-1): Remember to <u>reverse</u> the order!

Multiply by -1:

$$(-1)(-3 < p < +3 \quad) \quad =$$
$$(-1)(-3) > (-1)(p) > (-1)(+3)$$

reverse order

So we get $+3 > -p > -3$

---

32. If $a < b$ then is $na < nb$?

<u>This is true only if $n > 0$ (or if n is positive).</u>

33. Average score is defined as total scores divided by number of students (or number of tests taken).

   In other words:

   Average Score $= \dfrac{\text{Total Score}}{\text{No. of Students (Tests)}}$

   Total Scores $= 45 + 60 + 90$
   $= 195$

   No. Students $= 3$

   So $\dfrac{195}{3}$ $= \underline{65}$

34. Average rate is defined as Total Distance divided by Total Time.

   So Average Rate $= \dfrac{\text{Total Distance}}{\text{Total Time}}$

   Since Total Distance was given as 30 miles and Time was 3 hours,

   Average Rate $= \dfrac{30}{3} = \underline{10 \text{ mph.}}$

Arm Yourself

Below are summaries of factors, equivalencies, exponents, roots, etc., that are frequently encountered on the SAT. You should arm yourself for the SAT by making sure you know them all. Know them literally backwards and forwards. Whenever you see just one side of any of these equations and equivalencies, the other side should immediately spring to mind. If you do not arm yourself with this material, you will not be able to use the math strategies effectively.

Factors

$$(a + b)^2 = a^2 + 2ab + b^2 \qquad\qquad (a - b)^2 = a^2 - 2ab + b^2$$

The expression $a^2 + b^2$ is not factorable into anything useful. But the expression $a^2 - b^2$ contains a very important pair of factors.

$$a^2 - b^2 = (a + b)(a - b) \qquad \text{(Don't confuse this with } (a - b)^2,$$
$$\text{above!)}$$

Here are examples of how $a^2 - b^2$ sometimes appears:

$$a^2 - 1 = (a + 1)(a - 1)$$
$$a^2 - 4 = (a + 2)(a - 2)$$
$$\text{etc.}$$

Notice how number pairs like the following, whose difference is an even number, fit the $a^2 - b^2$ pattern:

$$99 \times 101 = (100 + 1)(100 - 1) = 100^2 - 1$$
$$802 \times 798 = (800 + 2)(800 - 2) = 800^2 - 2^2$$

Watch out for these. They may fool you:

$(a + b)^2$ is not the same as $a^2 + b^2$ (See above)
$(a - b)^2$ is not the same as $a^2 - b^2$ (See above)

Square Roots

$$\sqrt{x}\,\sqrt{y} = \sqrt{xy}$$

$$(\sqrt{x} + \sqrt{y})^2 = x + 2\sqrt{xy} + y$$
$$(\sqrt{x} - \sqrt{y})^2 = x - 2\sqrt{xy} + y$$
$$(\sqrt{x + y})^2 = x + y$$
$$(\sqrt{xy})^2 = xy$$

- -

Be very careful of these. They may fool you.

$\sqrt{x} + \sqrt{y}$ is not equal to $\sqrt{x + y}$

$\sqrt{x} - \sqrt{y}$ is not equal to $\sqrt{x - y}$

$(\sqrt{x} + \sqrt{y})^2$ is not equal to $x + y$ (see above)

$(\sqrt{x} - \sqrt{y})^2$ is not equal to $x - y$ (see above)

. . . .

Exponents

$x^0 = 1$ $\qquad\qquad$ $x^1 = x$ (Both very important!)

$x^3 \cdot x^5 = x^{3+5} = x^8$ $\qquad$ (To multiply, add exponents)
$x^n \cdot x^m = x^{n+m}$

$\dfrac{x^n}{x^m} = x^{n-m}$ $\qquad$ (To divide, subtract exponents)

$(ab)^n = a^n \cdot b^n$
$(a^m)^n = a^{mn}$ $\quad$ (It does <u>not</u> equal a^{m+n})

Here are examples involving factoring with exponents. Study them carefully until you thoroughly understand them.

$2^7 - 2^6 = 2^6(2^1 - 2^0) = 2^6(2 - 1) = 2^6(1) = 2^6$
$10^7 - 10^6 = 10^6(10^1 - 10^0) = 10^6(10 - 1) = 10^6(9)$ or 9×10^6
$x^5 + x^3 = x^3(x^2 + x^0) = x^3(x^2 + 1)$
$x^5 - x^3 = x^3(x^2 - x^0) = x^3(x^2 - 1) = x^3(x + 1)(x - 1)$

Here's a very important equivalency involving exponents:

$a^{-x} = \dfrac{1}{a^x}$

Reciprocals

$$\frac{1}{\frac{a}{b}} = \frac{b}{a}$$

$$\frac{a}{\frac{b}{c}} = a \cdot \frac{c}{b} = \frac{ac}{b}$$

$$\frac{1}{\frac{1}{x}} = \frac{x}{1} = x$$

$$\frac{\frac{a}{b}}{c} = \frac{a}{b} \div c = \frac{a}{b} \times \frac{1}{c} = \frac{a}{bc}$$

$$\frac{1}{x} + \frac{1}{y} = \frac{x + y}{xy}$$

$$a^{-x} = \frac{1}{a^x}$$

$$\frac{x}{y} + \frac{y}{x} = \frac{x^2 + y^2}{xy}$$

....

Rates

rate X time = distance

$$r \times t = d \qquad r = \frac{d}{t} \qquad t = \frac{d}{r}$$

$$\text{Average rate} = \frac{\text{total distance}}{\text{total time}}$$

....

Odds and Evens

e = any even integer

o = any odd integer

$$\left.\begin{array}{c} o \pm o \\ e \pm e \end{array}\right\} = e \qquad o \times o = o \qquad \frac{o}{o} = o \text{ or a fraction}$$

$$\left.\begin{array}{c} o \pm e \\ e \pm o \end{array}\right\} = o \qquad \left.\begin{array}{c} e \times e \\ e \times o \end{array}\right\} = e \qquad \frac{o}{e} = \text{a fraction}$$

$$e^2 = e \\ o^2 = o \qquad\qquad\qquad\qquad \frac{e}{o} = e \text{ or a fraction}$$

$$\frac{e}{e} = e \text{ or } o \text{ or a fraction}$$

Signs

minus X minus } = plus   minus X plus } = minus
plus X plus }   plus X minus }

$$\frac{1}{x} = \frac{-1}{-x} = -\left(\frac{1}{-x}\right) = -\left(\frac{-1}{x}\right) \qquad -\left(\frac{1}{x}\right) = \frac{1}{-x} = \frac{-1}{x} = -\left(\frac{-1}{-x}\right)$$

....

Inequalities

$a > b$ means a is greater than b.

$a < b$ means b is greater than a (or a is less than b)

REMEMBER: THE OPEN MOUTH OF THE SYMBOL IS ON THE SIDE OF
THE <u>GREATER</u> QUANTITY

$a \leqq b$ means b is greater than or equal to a

$a < b < c$ means that the value of b is between a and c (or, b
is greater than a and c is greater than b)

$a \leqq b \leqq c$ means that the lowest possible value of b is a;
the highest possible value is c; and it may be anywhere in between

$0 < x < 1$ means that that x is a positive fraction less than
one

$a > b$ also means $b < a$

REGULAR MATH QUESTIONS

Before we illustrate strategies and shortcuts with specific SAT type examples, you ought to know some important math shortcuts. Here they are (strategies 29-33):

To find which of two fractions is larger, use the criss-cross multiplication method.

Many times you will find a question in which you must compare the values of two fractions. For example suppose you want to find which fraction is greater:

$$\frac{5}{13} \quad \text{or} \quad \frac{3}{8}$$

Many students would try to get a common denominator and then compare the fractions. That's the long way! Here's how to do it the short way, using the technique called <u>criss-cross</u> <u>multiplication</u> (multiplying the numerator of each fraction by the denominator of the other).

Multiply the 8 by the 5 and put the result under the 5/13. Then multiply the 13 by the 3 and put the result under the 3/8. Like this:

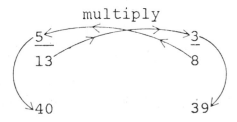

Since 40 is greater than 39, and 40 was under the 5/13, then 5/13 is greater than 3/8. This works every time, and of course you can prove this, but that's not our purpose here.

Notice how much more simple it is to compare fractions this way instead of getting a common denominator and then comparing them.

Remember, when you criss-cross multiply a denominator times a numerator, you must put your answer under the fraction whose numerator you used in multiplying. Remember it this way: <u>put your answer under the numerator</u>.

Try these examples. Which is greater?

(A) $\frac{7}{9}$ or $\frac{5}{7}$ (B) $\frac{3}{5}$ or $\frac{4}{7}$ (C) $\frac{11}{13}$ or $\frac{7}{8}$

Answers: $\frac{7}{9}$, $\frac{3}{5}$, $\frac{7}{8}$

To add or subtract fractions rapidly, use the criss-cross multiplication method.

Suppose you have the following problem: Find the value of $\frac{3}{4} + \frac{5}{6}$. Most people would try to find the common denominator and then add. Here's a shorter way when you don't want to get the common denominator.

$$\underset{\text{multiply}}{\overset{\text{multiply}}{\frac{3}{4} + \frac{5}{6}}} = \frac{3 \times 6 + 4 \times 5}{4 \times 6} = \frac{18+20}{24} = \frac{38}{24}$$

What we have done is to multiply the 6 by the 3, and add that result to the product of the numbers 4 by 5. The result is our answer's <u>numerator</u>. Then multiply the 4 by the 6 and the result is our answer's <u>denominator</u>. So our answer is:

$$\frac{38}{24} = \frac{19}{12} = 1\frac{7}{12}$$

77

If we want to subtract: $\frac{5}{7} - \frac{3}{10}$ we would do the following:

$$\overset{\text{multiply}}{\frac{5}{7} - \frac{3}{10}} = \frac{5 \times 10 - 7 \times 3}{7 \times 10} = \frac{50-21}{70} = \frac{29}{70}$$

multiply

Try these examples. Add the following fractions:

(A) $\frac{4}{5} + \frac{5}{7}$ (B) $\frac{7}{9} + \frac{3}{4}$ (C) $\frac{x}{y} + \frac{y}{x}$ (Remember this one!)

Answers:

(A) $\frac{53}{35}$ or $1\frac{18}{35}$ (B) $\frac{55}{36}$ or $1\frac{19}{36}$ (C) $\frac{x^2 + y^2}{xy}$

Try these now. Subtract:

(A) $\frac{2}{3} - \frac{1}{2}$ (B) $\frac{3}{4} - \frac{1}{7}$ (C) $\frac{x}{y} - \frac{y}{x}$

Answers: $\frac{1}{6}$, $\frac{17}{28}$, $\frac{x^2 - y^2}{xy}$ or $\frac{(x + y)(x - y)}{xy}$ (by factoring)

STRATEGY 31

To find the sale price in discount problems, start by subtracting the discount % from 100%.

Sometimes you have to figure what selling price you would pay for an item discounted a certain percent. Here's an example:

What is the selling price of an article that lists for $5.00 and is discounted 20%?

Most of you would probably multiply 20% by $5.00 and then subtract that result from $5.00. There's a faster way.

First, always <u>subtract the percent from 100%</u>. In this case you would subtract 20% from 100% and get 80%. Now multiply this 80% by the $5.00. You get $4.00, and that's the answer.

So, in summary, subtract the percent discount from 100%, then multiply that number by the list price to get the sale price.

Try these examples:

1. What is the selling price of an item discounted 30% whose list price (before discount) is $8.00?

2. What is the selling price of an item discounted 40% whose list price is $4.00?

Answers: 1. $5.60; 2. $2.40

STRATEGY
32

To turn a fraction into a percent, try multiplying instead of dividing.

Suppose you have a number like 3/25 and want to find what percent that is. You may be tempted, as most students are, to divide 25 into 3. That sure is the long way! Now just do some thinking: Isn't it easier to work with simple denominators than hard ones? So let's make the denominator 25 into a simpler one. We can do this by multiplying 25 by 4 to get 100. But since you are going to multiply the denominator by 4 you must also multiply the numerator, 3, by 4 so you don't change the value of the fraction! Like this:

$$\frac{3}{25} \times \frac{4}{4} = \frac{12}{100}$$

Thus we get 12/100 which is just 12%. That's our answer.

This method works on fractions with any of the following denominators:

2, 4, 5, 10, 20, 25, 50

Try these examples. Write each of the following fractions as a percent (or as an integer over 100):

(A) $\frac{1}{2}$ (B) $\frac{1}{4}$ (C) $\frac{2}{5}$ (D) $\frac{3}{10}$ (E) $\frac{3}{20}$ (F) $\frac{4}{25}$ (G) $\frac{1}{50}$

Answers: (A) 50% or $\frac{50}{100}$ (E) 15% or $\frac{15}{100}$

(B) 25% or $\frac{25}{100}$ (F) 16% or $\frac{16}{100}$

(C) 40% or $\frac{40}{100}$ (G) 2% or $\frac{2}{100}$

(D) 30% or $\frac{30}{100}$

STRATEGY
33

Work with addition instead of subtraction.

Just as before you saw that it is simpler sometimes to _multiply instead of to divide_, you'll find that many times it is simpler to _add instead of to subtract_.

Here's an example: Which is greater, $\frac{7}{12} - \frac{1}{13}$ or $\frac{6}{13}$?

Most students would subtract the $\frac{7}{12} - \frac{1}{13}$. That's _not_ the best way. Let's write the comparison under two columns, A and B. (You'll find this particularly useful in quantitative comparison questions.)

Column A	Column B
$\frac{7}{12} - \frac{1}{13}$	$\frac{6}{13}$

Let's <u>add</u> $\frac{1}{13}$ to both columns to get rid of the minus sign. We can do this without changing the order of the columns because we are adding the <u>same thing</u> to both columns. So we get

Column A	Column B
$\frac{7}{12}$	$\frac{6}{13} + \frac{1}{13}$

Now Column A is just 7/12 and Column B is 7/13. It is easy to see that 7/12 is greater than 7/13 since the denominator of 7/12 is smaller. So we find that Column A is greater than Column B; and since Column A was originally 7/12 - 1/13 and Column B was originally 6/13, 7/12 - 1/13 is greater than 6/13.

You may think that the numbers in this problem were specially chosen to support our strategy, but in every case that I have seen, this is the type of question that the test makers use on this SAT exam.

Notice we didn't have to spend time getting a common denominator, which would mean multiplying the 12 by the 13 (and also the 13 by the 7). Now here's how you can even use this method in a geometry type question, which is the way the SAT would vary the preceding problem.

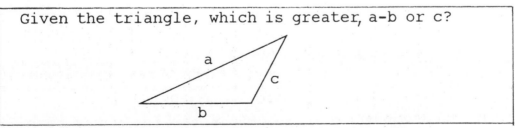

Given the triangle, which is greater, a-b or c?

Again put the a-b and the c in two columns:

Column A	Column B
a-b	c

Many students would probably try to figure how the difference a-b compares with c. Here's the shortcut way: Get rid of the minus sign. Add b to both columns. We get:

Column A	Column B
a	b + c

Now isn't it obvious that side a is <u>less</u> than the sum of sides b and c (the shortest distance between two points is a straight line --or if you remember, the sum of two sides of a triangle is greater than the remaining side). So we find that Column A is less than Column B, and so a-b (which was originally under Column A) is <u>less</u> than c (which was originally under Column B).

The reason why working with addition is faster than working with subtraction has to do with the fact that the process of subtraction was developed from the process of addition, and therefore addition is more <u>fundamental and basic and therefore more natural to work with</u>. The same thing works for multiplication-division. That is, it is usually better to work with multiplication than division. So here again you would try to get rid of the complicated divisor by somehow performing a multiplication operation. I'll show you more on this later.

STRATEGY
34

Read math questions very carefully, so that you solve for what is asked for.

Telling you to read questions carefully may seem like an obvious piece of advice. But SAT questions often seem to ask for one thing while actually asking for another. For example:

If a is not 0 or 1 and b is not 0 or 1,
what is the reciprocal of $\dfrac{1}{\frac{1}{a} + \frac{1}{b}}$?

(A) $\dfrac{ab}{a + b}$ (B) $\dfrac{1}{a + b}$ (C) $a + b$ (D) ab (E) $\dfrac{a + b}{ab}$

If you are not careful, you might simplify the expression $\dfrac{1}{\frac{1}{a} + \frac{1}{b}}$ and get the answer $\dfrac{ab}{a + b}$, Choice A. That's the

correct simplification of the expression. And it's the wrong answer. The question asked for the <u>reciprocal</u> of the expression. And so the correct answer is Choice E. Many students get tricked because they either don't notice that the question asks for a reciprocal, or they forget after they have simplified the expression. Don't get so rushed that you do the math correctly but put down the wrong answer!

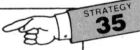

If you must test *all* choices, work from Choice E backwards.

Many questions ask you to work through many of the choices before coming to the correct one. And many students would start with Choice A first. Is that the best approach? Here's an example:

Which fraction is less than $\dfrac{2}{3}$?

(A) $\dfrac{3}{4}$ (B) $\dfrac{13}{19}$ (C) $\dfrac{15}{22}$ (D) $\dfrac{9}{13}$ (E) $\dfrac{7}{11}$

In this question, where you essentially have to <u>look through</u> the choices and cannot necessarily zero in on the correct choice, the test maker will expect you to work through Choices A, B, C, etc. in that order. And the chances are that if you're careless, you'll make a mistake before you get to the right choice. That's how the test maker makes up the choices. So, in cases such as this, start with Choice E and work backwards with Choice D, C, etc., in that order. The chances are that Choice E or D is the correct answer! So in the above question let's compare 2/3 with 7/11 in Choice E. Remember our shortcut way?

MULTIPLY

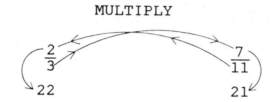

Since 22 is greater than 21, 2/3 is greater than 7/11; and so Choice E is in fact the correct answer.

Here's another SAT type question which involves the same strategy:

> If p is an even integer and q is an odd integer, which of the following could be an even integer?
>
> (A) q - p   (B) q + p   (C) $\frac{p + q}{2}$
>
> (D) $\frac{q}{2}$ + p   (E) $\frac{p}{2}$ + q

Note the word <u>could be</u> in the question. So, we just have to find one set of numbers which makes the choice an even number. Again, work <u>with Choice E first</u>. Since p is even, let p = 2 (for example). Since q is odd, let q = 3 (for example). Then Choice E, which is p/2 + q, becomes 2/2 + 3 = 1 + 3 = 4. So we see that Choice E <u>could be even</u>, and so it is the correct answer.

So remember, when you have to work with all the choices or have to substitute numbers in the choices (that is, when you cannot just arrive at a correct answer without looking through all the choices) <u>work with Choice E first</u>, then Choice D, etc., in that order. Chances are that Choice E or Choice D is correct.

STRATEGY
36

Use the "Translation Technique" on verbal problems to turn words into math symbols.

A verbal problem is simply a question in which you must translate words into mathematical terms. Many students have difficulty with such problems. Here's a way to make them quite simple and direct. If you master this technique, you should be able to do most verbal problems almost mechanically, with very little anxiety and brain-racking. We call this the <u>Translation Technique</u>.

Here's a typical SAT type question measuring verbal abilities in mathematics:

> John is three times as old as Paul, and Paul is two years older than Sam. If Sam is y years old, find an expression for the age of John.
>
> (A)   6 - 3y
> (B)   6 + 3y
> (C)   3y + 2
> (D)   3y - 2
> (E)   3y - 6

The key thing to remember about verbal problems is to translate the <u>key words</u>:

> <u>is</u> becomes =
>
> <u>of</u> becomes X (times)
>
> <u>more than</u>, <u>older than</u>, etc. becomes +
>
> <u>less than</u>, <u>younger than</u>, etc. becomes -
>
> % becomes $\dfrac{}{100}$
>
> <u>What</u> becomes x, y etc.

So let's look at the first part of the question:

"John is three times as old as Paul..."

This translates (with John = J, and P = Paul) as

(1)   J = 3 X P

The next part, "and Paul is two years older than Sam..."is translated as (Let S = Sam or Sam's age):

(2)   P = 2 + S

Now look at the second sentence: "If Sam is y years old, find an expression for the age of John." We translate this as:

S = y

Now substitute S = y into Equation (2) above:

We get: P = 2 + y.   Now substitute P = 2 + y into Equation (1). We get:

$$J = 3 \text{ X } P = 3 \text{ X } (2 + y) = 3 \text{ X } 2 + 3 \text{ X } y$$
$$= 6 + 3y$$

Thus, Choice B is correct.

Here's another typical verbal SAT-type problem:

Bill bought 4 times as many apples as Harry and 3 times as many apples as Martin. If Bill, Harry and Martin purchased less than a total of 200 apples, what is the greatest number of apples that Bill could have purchased?

(A)   168   (B)   180   (C)   120

(D)   110   (E)   90

Translate: The number of apples that Bill bought = B,

The numer of apples that Harry bought = H

The number of apples that Martin bought = M

The phrase "Bill bought 4 times as many apples as Harry" is translated to:

(1) B = 4 X H

The phrase "...and three times as many apples as Martin" is translated to:

$$(2) \quad B = 3 \times M$$

The phrase "If Bill, Harry, and Martin purchased less than a total of 200 apples..." is translated to:

$$(3) \quad B + H + M < 200$$

Now the question asks for the greatest number of apples that Bill could have purchased. Translated, it asks for the <u>maximum value of the variable B</u>. So let's just get some equation involving B and get rid of the H and the M. We can do this by substituting what H is in terms of B and what M is in terms of B in Equation (3).

That is, from Equation (1) we have: $B = 4H$ or $B/4 = H$, and from Equation (2) we have $B = 3M$ or $B/3 = M$. Now look at Equation (3): $B + H + M < 200$. Substitute $B/4 = H$ and $B/3 = M$:

$$B + \frac{B}{4} + \frac{B}{3} < 200$$

Factor:
$$B \left(1 + \frac{1}{4} + \frac{1}{3}\right) < 200$$

or
$$B \left(\frac{12}{12} + \frac{3}{12} + \frac{4}{12}\right) < 200$$

$$B \left(\frac{19}{12}\right) < 200$$

Get the B alone (multiply both sides of the inequality by 12 and divide by 19):

$$B < \frac{200 \times 12}{19}$$

B is less than $\frac{200 \times 12}{19}$. For simplicity, choose the greatest value of B as $\frac{200 \times 12}{20}$ since this number is just slightly less than $\frac{200 \times 12}{19}$. Thus the greatest value of

$B = \frac{200 \times 12}{20} = 120$. The answer is thus, Choice C.

In problems with more than one unknown, take special care with substitutions.

Sometimes you will have to substitute numbers or variables in a problem with two unknowns. It is very important for you to make the right substitution -- one that will lead you rapidly to the correct answer. In general, substitute to get rid of the unknown that is <u>not</u> part of the answer that the question asks for.

Let's look at another SAT-type verbal problem:

Mat and Phil have combined salaries of $1500 a week. Mat's salary is three-fifths Phil's. What is four-fifths of Mat's salary per week?

(A) $250.00   (B) $350.00   (C) $450.00
(D) $500.00   (E) $550.00

Make sure that you immediately write M for Mat, P for Phil (you can of course use m and p). The first sentence translates to

(1) $M + P = 1500$

The second sentence translates to

(2) $M = \frac{3}{5} P$

The question asks you to find the value of:

(3) $\frac{4}{5} M$

Since the second equation tells you that $M = \frac{3}{5} P$, you may be tempted to substitute $\frac{3}{5} P$ for M in the first equation and solve from there. Don't do it! Remember, the question asks you to find the value of $\frac{4}{5}$ <u>M</u>. Since we want to find the value of $\frac{4}{5} M$, let's get rid of P in the equations, and keep the M.

The best way to do this is to write P in terms of M in Equation (2):

$$M = \frac{3}{5}P; \quad 5M = 3P; \quad \text{so } \frac{5M}{3} = P$$

Then substitute $P = \frac{5M}{3}$ into Equation (1):

$$M + P = 1500; \quad M + \frac{5M}{3} = 1500;$$

$$\frac{3M + 5M}{3} = 1500; \quad \frac{8M}{3} = 1500$$

Now let's get the M alone by multiplying the last equation by 3/8:

$$\frac{8M}{3} \times \frac{3}{8} = 1500 \times \frac{3}{8}$$

$$M = 1500 \times \frac{3}{8}$$

We have to find the value of $\frac{4}{5}M$, so we multiply the last equation by $\frac{4}{5}$:

$$\frac{4}{5} \times M = 1500 \times \frac{3}{8} \times \frac{4}{5} = \overset{\overset{150}{\cancel{300}}}{\cancel{1500}} \times \frac{3}{\underset{\underset{1}{2}}{8}} \times \frac{\overset{1}{4}}{\underset{1}{5}} = 450$$

So, Choice C is correct.

STRATEGY
38

In solving a problem with several parts, start with the part that gives you the most information.

The worst thing you can do on the SAT is to exhaust yourself by thinking too hard on a particular question. Many times you will see a question that you know there is a definite answer for, but you also know that it will take you a long time to solve it. Furthermore, you may really rack your brains trying to solve the question. In every case

that I have seen, there's a fast, almost mechanical way to
do such problems. Here's a typical problem:

If $mnq = 0$, $mcr = 0$ and $nrc = 1$, which must be necessarily 0?
(A) n   (B) r   (C) m   (D) q   (E) c

Take a quick look at the first two equations: $mnq = 0$
and $mcr = 0$. You should immediately notice that <u>any or all</u>
of the unknowns could be 0. Not much information there!
Now go to the third equation: $nrc = 1$. This tells us that
neither n, r, nor c can be 0. Now with this information,
you can go back to Equation 2: $mcr = 0$. What you learned
from Equation 3 tells you that c and r cannot be 0, so m
must be. The correct answer is Choice C -- and you didn't
even need Equation 1 to find it!

Incidentally, don't jump to the conclusion that since
m is common to Equations 1 and 2, then $m = 0$. Your answer
would be right -- but for the wrong reason. In Equation 1,
q might have been 0 and in Equation 2, r might have been 0.
Only by going to Equation 3 can you see that r, c, and n
<u>cannot</u> be 0. (q could still be 0, but it doesn't have to
be.)

Here's another SAT question where you want to go right
away to the information that lets you start off the problem.

If $0.1 \leq m \leq 1$
and $0.001 \leq n \leq 0.01$
then the maximum value of $\frac{m}{n}$ is

(A) 1   (B) 10   (C) 100   (D) 1000   (E) 10,000

After reading through the question, look for the piece
of information you must use first. Note when reading the
statements that the information contained in them alone does
not enable us to start the problem. There is additional
"information" hidden in the question. To get the maximum

value of $\frac{m}{n}$, you must look for the greatest value of m and the least value of n. That is what will make the fraction $\frac{m}{n}$ greatest. So m must be 1 and n must be .001.

$$\frac{m}{n} = \frac{1}{.001} = \frac{1}{\frac{1}{1000}} = 1 \times \frac{1000}{1} = 1000$$

Choice D is correct.

STRATEGY
39

To find irregular or unusual lengths, areas, or volumes, try subtracting from a quantity you know or can calculate.

Let's look at another example:

In the above figure, Circle A has a radius of a and Circle B has a radius of b. What is the area of the region which is shaded?

(A) $\Pi (a + b)$ (B) $\Pi (b - a)$ (C) $\Pi (b^2 - a^2)$

(D) $\Pi (b^2 + a^2)$ (E) $\Pi (b - a)^2$

You can see that the area of the shaded region is just the <u>difference of the area of the big circle</u> (radius b) <u>and</u> <u>the area of the small circle</u> (radius a). The area of the small circle is just a^2, and the area of the big circle is just b^2. So the difference is:

$$\Pi b^2 - \Pi a^2 = \Pi (b^2 - a^2) \quad \text{(Choice C)}$$

Some questions ask you to subtract two <u>lengths</u> in order to find the unknown length. Here's an example:

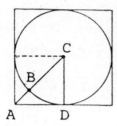

A circle is inscribed in the square above. Point C is the center of the circle. What is the ratio of AB to AC?

(A) $\dfrac{2 - \sqrt{2}}{2}$ (B) $\dfrac{\sqrt{2} + 1}{\sqrt{2}}$ (C) $\dfrac{\sqrt{2}}{2}$ (D) $\dfrac{2}{\sqrt{2}}$ (E) Cannot be determined

In the diagram above, call AB = s and the radius of the circle, r. Since CB is also the radius, CB = r. You should also realize that triangle ADC is an isosceles right triangle, and that therefore AD = r. Therefore side CA = $r\sqrt{2}$ (by the Pythagorean theorem).

We want to find what the ratio s to r + s is but we don't know what s is. Here's the main strategy:

SUBTRACT LINES FROM LINES TO GET UNKNOWN LINES.

CA - CB = BA (unknown)   noting that BA = s.
But CA = $r\sqrt{2}$ (from before) and CB = r
So CA - CB = $r\sqrt{2}$ - r
and since CA - CB = s,
    s = $r\sqrt{2}$ - r
So the ratio, $\dfrac{s}{r + s} = \dfrac{r\sqrt{2} - r}{r + r\sqrt{2} - r}$

(substituting $r\sqrt{2}$ - r for s in $\dfrac{s}{r + s}$)

The r's cancel and we get

$$\frac{r\sqrt{2} - r}{r + r\sqrt{2} - r} = \frac{\sqrt{2} - 1}{1 + \sqrt{2} - 1} = \frac{\sqrt{2} - 1}{\sqrt{2}}$$

But what? There's no answer in the choices like that! What do we do now? Don't panic -- and above all, don't choose Choice B just because it looks sort of like your answer with only one sign changed! Simplify your fraction by getting rid of $\sqrt{2}$ in the denominator. Multiply both numerator and denominator above by $\sqrt{2}$ to simplify the fraction. We get:

$$\left(\frac{\sqrt{2}-1}{\sqrt{2}}\right)\frac{\sqrt{2}}{\sqrt{2}} = \frac{\sqrt{2}\sqrt{2}-\sqrt{2}}{\sqrt{2}\sqrt{2}} = \frac{2-\sqrt{2}}{2}$$

Choice A is then correct.

Beware of "Average Rate" problems! Don't average rates. Divide total distance by total time.

"Average Rate" problems are very tricky. Here's a typical example:

> What is the average rate of a car initially travelling at 20 miles per hour and then travelling twice the initial distance at 60 miles per hour?
>
> (A) 40 mph   (B) 25 mph   (C) 30 mph
> (D) 36 mph   (E) 50 mph

Some students would be lured into thinking that they should average 20 and 60 to get 40 which is just Choice A. Or some may be lured into thinking that they should divide 60 by 2 because of the word "twice" and then average that result with 20 to get 25 which is just Choice B. But here's the method: <u>average rate</u> is <u>total distance divided by total time</u>:

<u>TOTAL DISTANCE</u>
TOTAL TIME

Now what is the total distance? Since distance is not given in the question let's just pick a value for initial distance. Since we have numbers like 20 and 60 in the question, let's choose the initial distance as a simple multiple of 20, like 20. This will make things simpler when you calculate. Let's proceed to find the TOTAL DISTANCE traveled. The initial distance (which we chose) is 20 miles. The car then traveled twice that distance. This means that the car next traveled 20 X 2 = 40 miles. So the TOTAL DISTANCE is 20 + 40 = 60 miles. Now let's find out what the TOTAL TIME is. If the car travelled 20 miles at 20 mph, the initial time would be

$$\frac{\text{initial distance}}{\text{initial rate}} = \frac{20 \text{ miles}}{20 \text{ miles per hour}} = 1 \text{ hour}$$

The final time would be

$$\frac{\text{final distance}}{\text{final rate}} = \frac{40 \text{ miles}}{60 \text{ miles per hour}} = \frac{4}{6} \text{ hours}$$

So the TOTAL TIME would be initial time + final time =

$$1 + \frac{4}{6} \text{ hours}$$

And now we may calculate the average rate:

$$\frac{\text{TOTAL DISTANCE}}{\text{TOTAL TIME}} = \frac{60 \text{ miles}}{1 + 4/6 \text{ hrs}} = \frac{60}{\frac{10}{6}} = 60 \text{ X } \frac{6}{10} = 36 \text{ mph}$$

Therefore the correct answer is Choice D.

In averaging scores, make sure that you separate terms out in order to use information on averages.

REMEMBER THAT THE AVERAGE IS EQUAL TO THE SUM OF THE SCORES DIVIDED BY THE NUMBER OF SCORES (TESTS OR STUDENTS).

Let's look at another "average" problem:

The average exam score, y, of a class of 20 students was below 68. If 8 students had increased their exam scores by 10 points each, the average exam score of the class would have been 68 or over. Which of the following describes the values of y?

(A) $56 \leq y < 68$

(B) $64 = y < 68$

(C) $64 < y < 68$

(D) $64 \leq y < 68$

(E) $64 \leq y \leq 68$

Now there is a really tricky way to do this problem based on the choices. I'll show you this way now, but I'd prefer you learn the honest way so that you may do many more problems based on the actual strategy.

FIRST METHOD: It seems pretty obvious that the choices one should consider are B,C,D, and E. Choice A with the 56 in there looks like a "dark horse," and the chances are that if 56 was in the answer, it would also be in the many of the other choices. Now look at the first statement in the question: It says that the score, y, was below 68. This means mathematically that $y < 68$. So already, we see that the only correct possibilities are Choices B,C, and D. Now the phrase "the average exam score would have been <u>68 or over</u>," gives a feeling that we have a <u>greater/equal sign</u> ($\geq$ or $\leq$) because of the words "68 or over." The only choice that fits the bill (from B,C, or D) is Choice D.

SECOND METHOD: Let's see how a knowledge of <u>separation of</u> <u>terms</u> would help solve this problem.

Let T stand for the total of all the class's exam scores. Then y (the average score) is T divided by 20 students:

$$\frac{T}{20} = y$$

If 8 students had increased their exam scores by 10 points each, the new total score would be:

$$T + (8 \times 10) = T + 80$$

And the new average score would be:

$$\frac{T + 80}{20}$$

Here's where the <u>separation of terms</u> strategy comes in. We can separate this last expression as follows:

$$\frac{T + 80}{20} = \frac{T}{20} + \frac{80}{20}$$

$$= \frac{T}{20} + 4$$

And since we know already that $\frac{T}{20} = y$

$$\frac{T + 80}{20} = y + 4 \quad \text{(substituting y for } \frac{T}{20}\text{)}$$

This expression, y + 4, is the <u>new</u> average score (when 8 students increase their score by 10 points each).

The problem states that the new average score is 68 or over. In mathematical terms:

$$y + 4 \geqq 68$$

Subtract 4 from both sides of the inequality/equality:

$$y + 4 - 4 \gtreqless 68 - 4$$
$$y \gtreqless 64 \ (\text{or}, \ 64 \lesseqgtr y)$$

Since the problem stated that $y < 68$, we combine inequalities to get:

$$64 \leqq y < 68$$

Thus choice D is correct.

The key to solving this problem is the knowledge that the expression $\frac{T + 80}{20}$ can be separated into $\frac{T}{20} + \frac{80}{20}$. This may at first seem like a rather unimportant point to make into a strategy. But this type of problem, involving an increase (or decrease) in an average, is one of the commonest type of SAT problems. Master this one strategy, and you'll probably add at least 10 points to your SAT score.

Be constantly on the lookout for standard, "classic" factors or similar equivalencies.

A very large number of SAT math questions are designed so that they can be solved by factoring or by writing an expression in another form. Sometimes this method gives you a shortcut way to a quick solution. Sometimes it is the only way to solve a problem. For example:

If $2 \leqq x \leqq 3$
   $1 \leqq y \leqq 4$

What is the maximum possible value of $\frac{x + y}{xy}$?

(A) $\frac{7}{12}$ (B) $\frac{3}{2}$ (C) $\frac{5}{4}$ (D) $\frac{4}{3}$ (E) $\frac{6}{8}$

Lots of students, seeing the word <u>maximum</u> in the problem, would rush ahead and substitute the maximum values of $x(3)$ and $y(4)$ in the expression $\frac{x + y}{xy}$. They would come up with Choice A as the answer. Don't do this! As you will see, it's wrong.

Look at the expression $\frac{x + y}{xy}$. And notice that it is the equivalent of the expression $\frac{1}{x} + \frac{1}{y}$. (Remember --
$$\frac{x + y}{xy} = \frac{x}{xy} + \frac{y}{xy} = \frac{1}{y} + \frac{1}{x}.)$$

To make a fraction as large as possible, make its denominator a small number. So you should substitute the <u>smallest</u> possible values of x and y to get the largest value of $\frac{1}{x} + \frac{1}{y}$:

$$\frac{1}{2} + \frac{1}{1} = 1\frac{1}{2} \text{ or } \frac{3}{2}$$

So the correct answer is Choice B.

Here's another example of the factoring strategy:

> If $x > 0$ and $x^2 - 1 = 246 \times 248$
> Then $x =$
>
> (A) 245   (B) 246   (C) 247   (D) 248   (E) 249

First off, you can virtually ignore the expression $x > 0$. Reason 1: There's no useful information there. Reason 2: It's just put in because the test maker didn't want to get into problems with zeros and minus values.

Go to the expression $x^2 - 1$. You should immediately notice that it can be factored into $(x + 1)(x - 1)$. Can the other half of the equation be expressed in the same way?

The answer is, of course, yes, it can:

$$246 \times 248 = (247 - 1)(247 + 1)$$

Therefore x is 247, and the correct answer is (C).

Notice that whenever a pair of multiplier numbers differs by an **even number** (e.g., 246 differs from 248 by 2), then there exists the possibility of factoring them in the way shown above.

Here's a final example of this very important strategy:

If $999 \times 1001 = 10^n - x$
where n is an integer, the pair
n, x could be:

(A) 3,2 (B) 6,3 (C) 6,1 (D) 3,1 (E) none of these

Note that the numbers 999×1001 are separated by 2. There's your clue, right there:

$$999 \times 1001 = (1000 + 1)(1000 - 1)$$

And, since $1000 = 10^3$, you can substitute:

$$(1000 + 1)(1000 - 1) = (10^3 + 1)(10^3 - 1)$$

Multiply the last expression out. Remember -- to multiply, add exponents.

$$(10^3 + 1)(10^3 - 1) = 10^6 - 1$$

And your answer is C, the pair 6,1.

When a question asks you to find a *compound* expression (like x + 1, or y/3, or a² +b²), look for a way to find this compound expression directly from what is given.

Sometimes an SAT math question asks you to find a quantity like x - 1 instead of x, or $\frac{y}{3}$ instead of y, or $a^2 + b^2$ instead of a and b. Whenever you are asked to find a compound expression like these, look for a way to find the expression directly. You want to avoid going through the trouble of finding the individual variables x, or y, or a, or whatever, and then constructing the compound expression from these variables.

Below are three powerful strategies for you to consider when faced with this type of problem. The problem will usually yield to one of the three.

Method 1: Try adding or subtracting quantities.

Look at the following example:

> If $3x + y = 7$ and $x + 3y = 13$,
> what is $x + y$?
>
> (A) 3   (B) 4   (C) 5   (D) 6   (E) 7

Don't solve for x or y! Try adding the two equations:

$$3x + y = 7$$
$$\underline{x + 3y = 13}$$
$$4x + 4y = 20$$

Dividing each expression by 4:

$$x + y = 5$$

So your answer is Choice C.

Method 2: Look for possible factors.

Here's a typical example:

> If $xy + 4y - x - 4 = 0$, and $x + 4 = -9$ then $y - 1 =$
> (A) +1   (B) +2   (C) 0   (D) -1   (E) -2

Here you can certainly solve for x and get $x = -13$ and then plug that value of $x = -13$ into the first equation, $xy + 4y - x - 4 = 0$ and then solve for y. Then you would calculate what y-1 is once you solved for the value of y. But ask yourself -- Why did the test maker give you what x + 4 was and not what x alone was? And, why did the test maker ask you to solve for y-1 and not just for y? I mean, you should be pretty sure that the test maker was not testing to see whether once you knew what y was you could solve for y - 1. So what I would do is to do something with the x + 4 and the y - 1. You should suspect that they are factors of something else you could use to solve the problem. Try multiplying them:

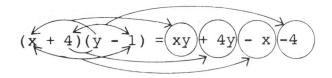

It turns out that x + 4 and y - 1, are the factors of the first equation in the problem! So therefore:

$$(x + 4)(y - 1) = 0$$

Since the two factors, multiplied together, equal 0, then one or both of the factors must equal 0. But the problem states that x + 4 = -9, not 0. So the other factor, y - 1, must be 0. Choice C is the correct answer.

Method 3: Expand out one of the expressions.

This is a third way of solving directly for the value of a compound expression. Look at the example:

> If $ab = -2$ and $(a + b)^2 = 8$, what is the value of $a^2 + b^2$?
>
> (A) 8   (B) 6   (C) 10   (D) 4   (E) 12

You first may be tempted to solve for the values of both a and b, and then substitute those values into the expression $a^2 + b^2$. That's some long way to do it. You should ask yourself -- If the test maker wanted you to find out what the value of a and b was, that is, if the test maker wanted you to solve for both a and b, the testmaker would have probably asked you to find the values of a and b and not a quantity like $a^2 + b^2$. So, you should think --Is there something that I can do with the quantities $ab = -2$ and $(a + b)^2 = 8$ so that I can somehow <u>produce</u> $a^2 + b^2$ from them? First, I would be tempted to expand out $(a + b)^2$:

$$(a + b)^2 = a^2 + 2ab + b^2 \quad \text{(Remember that relation?)}$$

Now $ab = -2$ so I substitute $ab = -2$ into the above:

$$(a + b)^2 = a^2 + 2(-2) + b^2$$

But $(a + b)^2 = 8$ (given), so

$$8 = a^2 + 2(-2) + b^2$$

and we get

$$8 = a^2 - 4 + b^2$$
$$12 = a^2 + b^2$$

So our answer is Choice E. Note why the first few choices are inserted.

Choice A is 8 because someone may think that
$(a + b)^2 = a^2 + b^2 = 8$.

Choice B is 6 because someone may just add: $8 + (-2)$.

Choice C is 10 because someone may subtract: $8 - (-2)$.

Choice D is 4 because in the last step of our solution above, when you bring the -4 over to the other side (in $8 = a^2 - 4 + b^2$) you may subtract $8 - 4$ to get 4.

Here's another SAT-type example of this strategy:

If $a + b = 4$ and $ab = 2$, what is the value of $a^2 + b^2$?

(A) 12   (B) 14   (C) 16   (D) 18   (E) 20

Expand out the equation $a + b = 4$ by squaring both sides. That will yield you an equation with the a^2 and the b^2 in it that you are looking for:

$$(a + b)^2 = 4^2$$
$$a^2 + 2ab + b^2 = 16$$

Now, if $ab = 2$ (the second equation in the problem), you can substitute:

$$a^2 + 2(2) + b^2 = 16$$

Now solve for $a^2 + b^2$:

$$a^2 + 4 + b^2 = 16$$
$$a^2 + b^2 = 16 - 4$$
$$= 12$$

And your answer is Choice A.

Simplify expressions by factoring out common quantities before you multiply.

Often, an equation in which compound expressions are multiplied can be solved by factoring out common quantities from each compound expression.

Here's an SAT-type example, using exponents for a change:

If $(2^7 - 2^6)(2^4 - 2^3) = 2^y$, then y =

(A) 6   (B) 7   (C) 8   (D) 9   (E) 10

Here you may be tempted to multiply

$$(2^7 - 2^6)(2^4 - 2^3)$$

But be a little observant: Factor out the 2^6 from the first factor.

We get $(2^7 - 2^6) = 2^6(2^1 - 2^0) = 2^6(2^1 - 1)$

> (remember you add exponents when multiplying)

Now factor out 2^3 from $(2^4 - 2^3)$

We get $(2^4 - 2^3) = 2^3(2^1 - 1)$

So we obtain $(2^7 - 2^6)(2^4 - 2^3) =$
$$2^6(2^1 - 1) \times 2^3(2^1 - 1)$$

But $2^1 = 2$ and since $2 - 1 = 1$, we find the above is just
$$2^6 \times 2^3$$

which is just 2^9 (add exponents)

Thus the relation,

$$(2^7 - 2^6)(2^4 - 2^3) = 2^y$$

is equal to 2^9 and
$$2^y = 2^9$$

so y = 9 and Choice D is correct.

Many times, factoring such as we did above, simplifies the solution tremendously.

STRATEGY
45

In problems containing unfamiliar symbols, use simple substitution.

From my experience, many students have problems with questions containing unfamiliar symbols. For example, here's a problem containing an unfamiliar symbol: a small square. This is not a standard math symbol at all. It is an arbitrary symbol invented by the test maker to express a particular relationship between the quantities A and B. However, symbols like these can be "translated" and used fairly easily:

> If for all real numbers, $A \square B = A^2 + B^2 - AB$, then what is the value of $(2 \square 3) \square 3$?
>
> (A) 18   (B) 6   (C) 108   (D) 64   (E) 37

All that $A \square B$ means is that every time you see a quantity on the left of the box (an A quantity) and a quantity on the right (a B quantity) you write the following:

$$A \square B = A^2 + B^2 - AB$$

Now the question asks what is $(2 \square 3) \square 3$?

Calculate what $(2 \square 3)$ is first, since this is inside the parentheses.

It is

$$(2 \square 3) = 2^2 + 3^2 - (2)(3) = 4 + 9 - 6 = 7$$

Now we are asked to find what $(2 \square 3) \square 3$ is. We know that $(2 \square 3) = 7$, so $(2 \square 3) \square 3 = 7 \square 3$. But $7 \square 3 = 7^2 + 3^2 - (7)(3) = 49 + 9 - 21 = 37$

Choice E is then correct.

Here's another SAT example of the same type. In this problem, the arbitrary symbol is $\emptyset$.

If x, y, z, m, n, q are all positive numbers and if $xyz \ \emptyset \ mnq = \dfrac{xyz}{mnq} + \dfrac{mnq}{xyz}$, then $xxy \ \emptyset \ xyz =$

(A) $\dfrac{zx}{mn}$ (B) $\dfrac{zx}{x^2 + y^2}$ (C) $\dfrac{zx}{x^2 + z^2}$

(D) $\dfrac{x^2 + z^2}{zx}$ (E) none of these

Now remember to substitute as shown in the diagram:

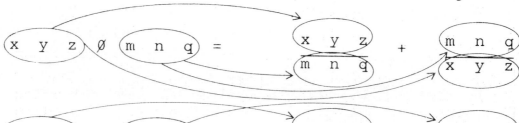

So

Now cancelling like terms:

$$\frac{\cancel{x}}{\cancel{x}} \cdot \frac{x}{\cancel{y}} \cdot \frac{\cancel{y}}{z} + \frac{\cancel{x}}{\cancel{x}} \cdot \frac{\cancel{y}}{x} \cdot \frac{z}{\cancel{y}} = \frac{x}{z} + \frac{z}{x}$$

But, what? There is no answer in the choice with the form $\frac{x}{z} + \frac{z}{x}$!

You may, at this point be tempted to choose Choice E (none of these), but what I'd do first is to add:

$$\frac{x}{z} + \frac{z}{x}$$

Remember the shortcut way?

$$\overset{\text{multiply}}{\underset{\text{multiply}}{\frac{x}{z} + \frac{z}{x}}} = \frac{x^2 + z^2}{zx}$$

So, $\dfrac{x}{z} + \dfrac{z}{x} = \dfrac{x^2 + z^2}{zx}$, which is just Choice D.

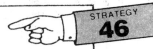

Try to get rid of fractions.

STRATEGY **46**

In many examples, you will not have to carry out a tedious solution but through common sense or logic, you can get an answer readily. Here's an SAT-type example:

---

a,b,c,d, and e are different integers. Each of the numbers is equal to one of the following numbers: 1,2,4,12,and 48. If $6a = \frac{1}{4}b = 12c = d = 3e$ then c =

(A) 48　　(B) 12　　(C) 4　　(D) 2　　(E) 1

107

The first thing to do is to simplify the numbers: Get rid of the fraction -- Remember to multiply instead of divide where you can - we went over this before. So I would try to get rid of the ¼ from ¼b. Since we want to find the value of c, we work with

$$\tfrac{1}{4}b = 12c$$

Multiply both sides of the above by 4. We get

$$b = 4 \times 12c = 48c$$

This says that b is 48 times another number c. Look at the numbers for a,b,c,d, and e: 1,2,4,12, and 48. <u>The only numbers such that one is 48 times another are the numbers 1 and 48.</u> So, b must be 48 and c must be 1! Thus Choice E is correct. This method is the most direct way of doing this problem and also the fastest way.

STRATEGY
47

When a question asks you to find an exception, look for some element common to four of the five choices. The choice *without* that element is your answer.

Here's a fairly common type of SAT question -- a question that asks you to find a choice that is <u>different</u> from all its neighbors:

> If the dimensions of a rectangular box are represented by the choices, which box has a <u>different</u> volume from the other four? The box that has dimensions
>
> (A) 5 by 8 by 12
> (B) 15 by 16 by 2
> (C) 3 by 32 by 5
> (D) 3 by 4 by 40
> (E) 2 by 6 by 36

There are three ways to do this problem, and one is better than the other. The worst way to do it would be to calculate all the volumes by multiplying the numbers in each of the choices. <u>Since you are looking for a choice that is</u> <u>different from the other four choices, there must be</u> <u>something in four of the choices that the correct choice</u> <u>doesn't contain.</u> One way of spotting the correct choice is to notice that Choices A,B,C, and D are such that the product of the numbers in each of those choices end in 0. Choice E's product does not. But the <u>best</u> way to notice the difference is to see that there is a 5 or you can get a 5 from each of the choices, A,B,C, or D, but there is no way to extract a five 5 from Choice E. Therefore Choice E is the answer. (Notice that if you had looked for 4's first, you wouldn't have found the answer!)

Note that in the above SAT example, for those that would calculate the product in each of the choices, they would probably go through all the first four choices before coming to the correct last one. So here the strategy would be to start with Choice E, first, in your calculations, and work backwards calculating the product in Choice D next, etc.

Look out for unnecessary information!

Many times there will be a question which presents information which you will use to solve the problem. However knowing the right strategy and approach, it is better not to make use of the "extraneous" information, (which I think is very unfair of the test-maker to present to you).

Here's an SAT-type example:

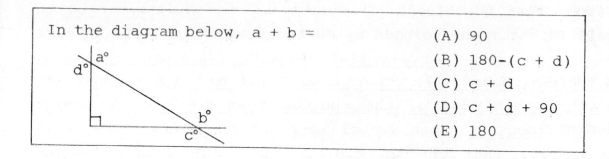

In the diagram below, a + b =

(A) 90

(B) 180-(c + d)

(C) c + d

(D) c + d + 90

(E) 180

Here the key strategy is to try to be observant and use the information that will give you the <u>fastest</u> result. If you use the fact that one of the angles of the triangle is 90°, you'll be playing around with angles and trying to figure them out. However, just look at the diagram. Aren't angles a and d vertical angles and aren't angles b and c vertical angles? So, a = d and b = c. Then a + b = c + d because equals added to equals are equal. So, Choice C is correct, and you really didn't have to calculate specifically what the angles were by using the fact that one of the angles of the triangle was 90°. So don't let the test-maker lure you into using unnecessary information or lead you on the wrong road by providing you with such information!

Here's another SAT-type example:

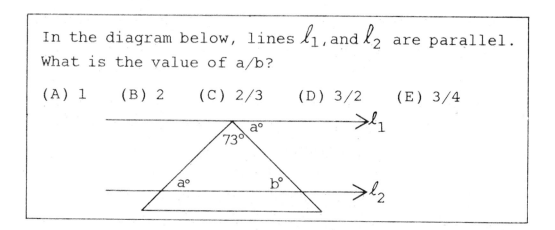

In the diagram below, lines ℓ_1, and ℓ_2 are parallel. What is the value of a/b?

(A) 1   (B) 2   (C) 2/3   (D) 3/2   (E) 3/4

Here you would be foolish to use the angle 73° and the angle a° in the triangle. You will spend too much time if you do, calculating angles. Instead look at the parallel lines. What do they tell you? Parallel lines tell you that a lot of angles are related and equal. For example they tell you that a° = b° (alternate interior angles of parallel lines are equal). Therefore a/b must be equal to 1! Choice A is the correct answer. And you didn't even need to use that strange angle 73° or the other angle a°!

"Round Off" amounts when a question asks you to approximate a quantity.

Some questions ask you to approximate a rather scary looking quantity. If you know the correct approach the problem becomes very simple. What you want to do is round off the denominators and represent all numbers as multiples of 10 where you can. For example:

Find the closest approximation to:

$$\frac{15,127,986}{2,965}$$

(A) 50   (B) 500   (C) 5000   (D) 50,000   (E) 500,000

First round off the denominator so division will be easier. Write 2965 as 3000. If you have to, round off the numerator. Write 15,127,986 as 15,000,000. Our rounded-off fraction is now approximated by

$$\frac{15,000,000}{3,000}$$

$$\frac{15,000,000}{3,000} = \frac{15000000}{3000} = \frac{15000}{3} = 5000.$$

Choice C is correct.

QUANTITATIVE COMPARISONS

On your SAT you will be given several questions of the type called Quantitative Comparison. Here you are presented with two columns, A and B, and you have to determine a relationship (if there is one) between the quantities in the columns. Here's an example. (Note this example is too simple for an actual SAT question and is used here only to illustrate the directions for this question type.)

Column A	Column B
2	-1

You would mark Choice A on your answer sheet if the quantity in Column A is always greater than the quantity in Column B.

You would mark Choice B on your answer sheet if the quantity in Column B is always greater than the quantity in Column A (or, saying it a different way, if the quantity in Column A is always less than the quantity in Column B).

You would mark Choice C on your answer sheet if the quantities in Columns A and B are always equal.

You would mark Choice D on your answer sheet if you cannot make a definite comparison of the two quantities-- for example, if the quantity in Column A is sometimes greater than and sometimes less than the quantity in Column B.

In the example on the previous page, Choice A is correct, since Column A $>$ Column B.

If something is in the middle of the columns, it refers to both columns and is sometimes called "the Given." Here's what I mean:

Column A	Column B
$x = 1$	
x - 1	x + 1

The middle expression can be read, "Given x equal to 1" or "If x equals 1."

To answer the question, we substitute $x = 1$ in both Columns A and B. Column A and B then become:

Column A	Column B
1 - 1 (=0)	1 + 1 (=2)

So the answer to this question is Choice B, since the quantity in Column A (x - 1) is less than the quantity in Column B (x + 1) when x = 1 (Given).

MAKE SURE THAT YOU MEMORIZE THESE DIRECTIONS FOR THE QUANTITATIVE COMPARISON QUESTION SO THAT ON YOUR ACTUAL SAT YOU DON'T HAVE TO REFER BACK TO THEM. That is, memorize that Choice A means Column A $>$ Column B, Choice B means that Column B $>$ Column A, etc.

Now here is the basic concept to remember when working with Quantitative Comparison questions. In most cases, the expressions in the two columns will be more or less complex.

They cannot be compared just at a glance. You will usually have to do something to them -- manipulate them mathematically in some way -- so that they look simpler and can easily be compared. The strategies in this section will show you how to do this.

STRATEGY 50

In doing trial substitutions, remember that x can be 0 or a negative quantity.

Don't be fooled by what at first looks like an easy comparison:

Column A	Column B
x	-x

Note that there is not a definite comparison between the columns: If x = 1 Column A = 1 and Column B = -1 and Column A $>$ Column B. But x might be a negative quantity! If x = -1, Column A = -1 and Column B = -(-1) = +1. In that case, Column B $>$ Column A. So a definite comparison cannot be made and Choice D is correct.

STRATEGY 51

You can multiply or divide both columns by the same *positive* number, and the relation between them will stay the same.

Multiplication (or division) is one common way of changing the quantities in the columns so that they can be compared. For example:

Column A	Column B
$\dfrac{17}{8}$	$\dfrac{7}{4}$

Multiply both columns by 8. You get:

$$\frac{17}{8} \times 8 \qquad\qquad \frac{7 \times 8}{4}$$

which becomes

17   14

So Column A $>$ B and you would pick Choice A.

WARNING: For this strategy to work, you must multiply or divide by a positive number. If you use a negative number, you reverse the relationship of the columns. For example:

Column A	Column B
7	3

Column A is obviously larger than Column B. But multiply by -1. Now you get:

-7   -3

And the relationship is reversed. Now B $>$ A.

You can add the same number to both columns (or subtract the same number from both columns) and the relationship between columns will stay the same.

STRATEGY
52

Adding or subtracting is another way of changing quantities so they are easily compared. (In most cases, adding is better.) For example:

Column A	Column B
$1 - \dfrac{1}{4}$	$\dfrac{3}{4} - \dfrac{1}{8}$

Add $\dfrac{1}{4}$ to both Columns: We get

Column A	Column B
1	$1 - \dfrac{1}{8}$

You can see that Column A $>$ Column B and so the correct answer would be Choice A.

Here's an SAT-type example of how much easier a comparison is when you simplify it by addition:

Column A	Column B
$\dfrac{7}{12} - \dfrac{1}{13}$	$\dfrac{6}{13}$

Instead of getting a common denominator and finding the <u>actual</u> value of Column A, let's add one-thirteenth to both sides (getting rid of tedious minus operations). The columns become:

Column A	Column B
$\dfrac{7}{12}$	$\dfrac{7}{13}$

SINCE 7/12 > 7/13, Column A > Column B and Choice A is correct.

Note that, unlike the multiplication/division strategy, you can use either positive or negative numbers here. (Subtracting, remember, is the same as adding a minus number!)

STRATEGY 53

When there are no unknowns (like x, y, a, b, etc.) in either column, never guess Choice D.

This is a quick, useful strategy. Where all quantities are known, some kind of definite comparison can always be made. So whenever you see nothing but numbers in both columns, never guess Choice D!

STRATEGY 54

Cancel identical quantities (Exception: never divide by a negative number.)

Always eliminate identical quantities in the columns to simplify the comparison. Let's look at an example:

Column A	Column B
$\sqrt{3} - 2$	$\sqrt{5} - 2$

Since -2 is COMMON to both columns get rid of it (we can legitimately do this by adding +2 to both columns). Thus we get

117

Column A	Column B
$\sqrt{3}$	$\sqrt{5}$

Since $\sqrt{3} < \sqrt{5}$, Column A $<$ Column B and Choice B is correct.

Here's where you should cancel like numbers in the columns when there is a straight multiplication in the SAT question: This is a typical SAT example:

Column A	Column B
21 X 22 X 23	22 X 20 X 24

Here you should cancel the 22 since it is <u>common</u> to both columns. You get:

Column A	Column B
21 X 23	20 X 24

You can see that 21 and 24 are divisible exactly by 3, so you should divide both columns by 3. You get:

Column A	Column B
7 X 23	20 X 8

Now, 7 X 23 = 161 and 20 X 8 = 160, so Column A $>$ Column B and thus Choice A is correct.

Get rid of square roots if you can.

Quantitative Comparison questions containing square roots frequently appear in the SAT. For example:

Column A	Column B
	$x > 0$
	$y > 0$
$\sqrt{x} + \sqrt{y}$	$\sqrt{x + y}$

Let's try to get rid of as many square roots as we can.

Square both sides:

Column A	Column B
$(\sqrt{x} + \sqrt{y})(\sqrt{x} + \sqrt{y})$	$\sqrt{x + y}\ \sqrt{x + y}$
$\sqrt{x}\sqrt{x} + 2\sqrt{y}\sqrt{x} + \sqrt{y}\sqrt{y}$	$x + y$
$x + 2\sqrt{y}\sqrt{x} + y$	$x + y$

Cancel the $x + y$ from both sides. We are left with:

Column A	Column B
$2\sqrt{y}\sqrt{x}$	0

Since Column A is greater than Column B, Choice A is correct.

Another example:

Column A	Column B
	$y > 0$
$\sqrt{y + 2}$	$\sqrt{y} + 2$

First let's simplify the columns by getting rid of the square root. We can do this by <u>squaring</u> both columns. We get:

STRATEGY 55

Column A	Column B
$(\sqrt{y} + 2)(\sqrt{y} + 2)$	$(\sqrt{y} + 2)(\sqrt{y} + 2)$
$= y + 2$	$= y + 4 + 2\sqrt{y} + 2\sqrt{y}$

Remember that $(\sqrt{y})(\sqrt{y}) = y$?

Now get rid of the <u>common</u> y in both columns. We get:

Column A	Column B
2	$4 + 2\sqrt{y} + 2\sqrt{y}$

And you can see that Column A $<$ Column B. Choice B is correct.

STRATEGY 56

First try addition, not subtraction, to simplify columns.

Try always to add rather than to subtract when working Quantitative Comparison questions.

Here's a familiar example:

Column A	Column B
$\dfrac{1}{12}$	$\dfrac{7}{25} - \dfrac{5}{24}$

Remember this method?

Whatever you do, don't subtract $\dfrac{5}{24}$ from $\dfrac{7}{25}$! Instead <u>add</u> $\dfrac{5}{24}$ to both columns to get rid of the $-$ sign. We get:

Column A	Column B
$\frac{1}{12} + \frac{5}{24}$	$\frac{7}{25}$

Since $\frac{1}{12} = \frac{2}{24}$, Column A becomes

$$\frac{2}{24} + \frac{5}{24} = \frac{7}{24}$$

and so we get for Column A and Column B:

Column A	Column B
$\frac{7}{24}$	$\frac{7}{25}$

and you can see that Column A $>$ Column B and so Choice
A is correct.

Where division is difficult, multiply!

STRATEGY
57

Whenever division looks tedious or difficult, try
multiplication. Remember when you saw that it was better
to multiply rather than to divide in simplifying fractions?
Well here's a typical SAT question that uses that strategy:

Column A	Column B
$a > b > 0$	
$\dfrac{a^2 + b^2}{a + b}$	$a + b$

Multiply both columns by a + b to get rid of the division sign! We get:

Column A	Column B
$a^2 + b^2$	$(a + b)(a + b)$

Remember that $(a + b)(a + b) = a^2 + 2ab + b^2$? So we get:

Column A	Column B
$a^2 + b^2$	$a^2 + 2ab + b^2$

Cancel the like terms, $a^2 + b^2$ from the columns and we find:

Column A	Column B
0	2ab

Now since we were given that $a > b > 0$, it must be that $2ab > 0$, because a is positive and b is positive. Thus Column B is greater than Column A and so Choice B is correct.

SO, WHEN IT SEEMS SIMPLER OR ADVANTAGEOUS, ALWAYS MULTIPLY INSTEAD OF DIVIDING (THAT IS GET RID OF THE DIVISION SIGN WHERE IT APPEARS SIMPLER TO DO SO). AND, ALWAYS ADD INSTEAD OF SUBTRACTING WHEN YOU CAN MAKE THE PROBLEM SIMPLER THAT WAY. THE COLUMNS WILL APPEAR SO MUCH SIMPLER AND THEY WILL BE MUCH EASIER TO WORK WITH.

To show that the relation between columns cannot be determined, use the "Equal-Unequal" Method.

Sometimes a quick look at a quantitative comparison question will suggest to you that the relations between columns cannot be determined. Here's a quick way of proving to yourself that your hunch is correct. Look at the example:

Column A	Column B
$x^2 + x$	$x^4 - x^2$

In a problem like the foregoing, where there is no "Given" information entered above the two columns <u>and</u> where there are algebraic expressions (like x, or x + 1, or y, y^2, etc.), there is a high probability that the relation between columns cannot be determined and the correct answer is Choice D. Therefore, a good strategy is to assume D is correct and try to prove it. Here's how:

Look for a number for x that will make the columns equal. Usually, that number will be 0, 1, or -1. Then find another number that will make the columns unequal, and you've proved your case.

In the example above, x = 0 makes the columns <u>equal</u>. x = 1 makes them <u>unequal</u> (Column A becomes 1 + 1 = 2, and Column B becomes 1 - 1 = 0). So your hunch is correct, and D is the answer.

If the "Equal-Unequal" Method doesn't work, try substitution using extreme values.

Sometimes, when testing for Choice D, we can't easily find a value to make both columns equal. For example:

Column A	Column B
x - 1	$x^2 - 5$

Try two numbers for x -- one very simple and low (like 0 or 1) and the other much higher (like 100).

First substitute 0 for x. Column A becomes -1; Column B becomes -5. So in this case A > B.

Now substitute 100 for x. Column A becomes 99. Column B becomes 10,000 - 5. Plainly in this case B > A. So Choice D has been proved correct.

If a question contains a Given, try changing the material in the columns to relate it to the Given (or vice versa).

If a quantitative comparison contains a Given expression (above and between the columns), chances are good that there will be a definite comparison possible. So instead of trying to prove Choice D, you might operate on the columns to relate them to the Given. For example:

Column A	Column B
$1 > m > 0$	
m	m^2

Divide both columns by m. We can do this without changing the relation between the columns since it is given that m is positive (m > 0). Therefore the columns become:

Column A	Column B
$1 > m > 0$	
$\dfrac{m}{m}$ (=1)	$\dfrac{m^2}{m}$ (=m)

So the Columns become:

Column A	Column B
$1 > m > 0$	
1	m

But we are given that $1 > m$ so it is apparent that Column A > Column B. Choice A is therefore correct.

In the above solution, you operated on the columns so that you could compare them to the Given. Sometimes you may want to reverse the process -- operating on the Given so you can compare it with the columns. Let's start with the same example:

Column A	Column B
$1 > m > 0$	
m	m^2

Multiply the Given by m (Note that m is not zero and not negative, since m > 0):

$$m(1 > m > 0) = m > m^2 > 0$$

And your answer is right there. Obviously A is correct.

(There's even a third way to attack this problem! The Given tells you that m is a positive fraction less than one. For all positive fractions less than one, squaring them les- sens their value. Try it with several fractions if you don't believe it. So m must be greater than m^2, and Choice A is correct.)

Here's another SAT-type example where you would do some- thing to the columns to get a resemblance to the Given:

Column A	Column B
35% of y = 50	
$17\frac{1}{2}\%$ of y	25

Note that if you multiply both columns by 2, you get what is in the Given. That is, if we multiply Column A and Column B by 2, we get:

Column A	Column B
35% of y = 50	
35% of y	50

Since it is given that 35% of y = 50, Column A = Column B. Choice C is correct. Note that you didn't have to calculate what y was from the Given and then have to plug it back into the quantities in the columns.

Now here's a second example of starting off by operat- ing on the Given instead of on the columns:

Column A	Column B
(a + b)(a - b) = 5	
a^2	$b^2 + 5$

Confronted with a Given, $(a + b)(a - b) = 5$, that looks like this, I would immediately change it to its equivalent, $a^2 - b^2 = 5$.

Then, subtracting b^2 from both columns gives us

$$a^2 - b^2 \qquad\qquad\qquad b^2 + 5 - b^2 \ (=+5)$$

Since the revised Given states that $a^2 - b^2 = 5$, you can substitute in Column A and obtain

$$5 \qquad\qquad\qquad\qquad 5$$

The two columns are equal. The corect answer is Choice C.

Don't waste time choosing between strategies.

Never spend too much time trying to figure out which is the best strategy or shortcut you need to solve a problem. If you think that there might be two ways and the first one that you come up with looks like it will enable you to quickly solve the problem, use it! Here's an example of a question where there will be two excellent ways for solution:

Column A		Column B
	$b \neq 0$	
ab		$\dfrac{a}{b}$

FIRST METHOD: Because a may be 0, we cannot get rid of the common variable a by dividing by a, so don't be tempted to do this! Use <u>extreme</u> values for b: If b is extremely large like b = 1,000,000, and a is 1, you can see that Column A is much greater than Column B. Now choose a very very small value for b with a still being 1. If b is very very small like b = 1/1,000,000, then Column A is very small and Column B is very large so in that case Column A is much smaller than Column B. In one case Column A > Column B and in the other, Column B > Column A. A definite comparison cannot be made, and so Choice D is correct.

SECOND METHOD: Find a set of values which make the columns equal. This would be a = 0, b ≠ 0. Can you find a set of values which would make the columns unequal? You can see that if a ≠ 0, practically any value of b would make the quantities unequal. So, since in one case the quantities are equal and in at least one other case they are not, a definite comparison cannot be made and Choice D is correct.

STRATEGY
62

Try common sense or logic before you try complicated math.

Sometimes you will find that logic or common sense alone will enable you to solve the problem in a real jiffy. Here's an example:

Column A	Column B
Area of a circle of radius 100	Surface area of a sphere of radius 100

Whatever you do, please don't try to calculate the surface area of a sphere of radius 100 (even if you know the formula!). Think of expanding the plane area of a circle by stretching it to make a surface of just half a sphere of radius 100. By stretching, the surface area of half the sphere will certainly be greater than the area of the circle. So certainly the surface area of the whole sphere will be greater than the area of the circle. Thus Choice B is correct.

Here's another example:

Column A	Column B
$m + 4n = 9$	
$3m - 3n = 7$	
m	n

Here it would be very foolish to solve for m and n because it would take you quite a time compared to a much faster way: Look at the second equation: You have to be observant though.

$$3m - 3n = 7$$

Since $7 > 0$, it is certainly true that

$$3m - 3n > 0$$

Divide by 3: $m - n > 0$

And we get: by adding n to both sides of the inequality:

$$m > n$$

Voila! Choice A is correct. And you didn't even have to work with the equation $m + 4n = 9$!

Factoring often makes comparisons possible.

Here's an example which involves factoring:

Column A	Column B
999 X 1001	1000 X 1000

Logic should tell you that the test maker probably does not expect you to multiply 999 X 1001, even though this can be done. Since this is a comparison problem, let's try to get the 999 to look like something with 1000 and the 1001 to look like something with 1000. Like this:

$$999 = 1000 - 1; \quad 1001 = 1000 + 1$$

Thus the columns become:

Column A	Column B
(1000 -1)(1000 + 1)	1000 X 1000

Now remember your math rules: $(a - b)(a + b) = a^2 - b^2$.

So, $(1000 - 1)(1000 + 1) = 1000^2 - 1$ and the columns become:

Column A	Column B
$1000^2 - 1$	1000^2

It is obvious now that Column B is greater than Column A, and so Choice B is correct.

When a comparison does not contain simple numbers like 0 or 1, and where there are no mathematical manipulations that would simplify the question, then the quantities are probably equal.

I have noticed that the strategy outlined above works in just about every case that is applicable on the SAT. The quantities in the columns are probably equal, and the correct answer is Choice C, when:

a)   The numbers in the columns are not very simple ones like 0, 1, etc. They are highly specific ones like 6, $\frac{2}{5}$, 49, etc.

b)   There is no apparent math manipulation or anything useful you can do with the columns or the Given. You <u>must</u> substitute and/or compute, working the problem out the hard way.

Let me show you a few examples, because there is a lot of logic to this method.

Here's the first example:

Column A	Column B
R = 2s + 3q + 5k	
s = 5, q = 3, R = 49	
k	6

Normally one would substitute s = 5, q = 3, and R = 49 into the equation, R = 2s + 3q + 5k. Then he/she would solve for k and compare the value of k with 6. Suppose you felt that you didn't have time to do this and just wanted to guess. In a case like the above, which normally involves a straight calculation, with no shortcut and where there is a particular number like 6 in one of the columns, Choice C is correct! That is, the Columns are equal. Why is Choice C correct? Here's the answer from the test-maker's point of view. <u>There is a reason why the test-maker chose the number 6 in Column B instead of another number.</u> Suppose that the test-maker chose 2. In calculating, you would find that k = 6. So if 2 were in Column B, you would say Column A is <u>greater</u> than Column B, since 6 > 2. And you would find that Choice A is correct. But what about all the students that found k = 3,4,5, or any number greater than 2 and <u>not</u> 6? They would also choose Choice A and be marked right! Thus the test-maker would defeat his goal for finding whether the student legitimately got the correct answer. However, if the test-maker chose the correct value for k, 6, in Column B, there would be only <u>one</u> way to get that answer. That is, if a student made a mistake or guessed, the student would either find his answer <u>greater than 6 or less than 6</u>, and choose Choice A or B and be legitimately marked wrong. Also if a student just guesses, it would be improbable that the student would choose k = 6, since there are an infinite number of other possible values for k. So from the test-makers point of view, this approach of having Choice C as an answer for these types of questions greatly prevents a student from arriving at the correct choice by guessing or miscalculating.

Let's look at another of the many examples where this Choice C is the answer:

Column A	Column B
Weight of 4 dozen grapefruits = 2 kg	
Weight of 3 dozen oranges = 2 kg	
Weight of 1 dozen grapefruits and 1 dozen oranges	$1 \frac{1}{6}$ kg

132

Note that this question involves a straight calculation, without shortcut and that there is a particular number in one of the Columns, mainly Column B = $1\frac{1}{6}$. Therefore Choice C is correct.

Here's another:

Column A		Column B
	$x = 1$	
	$y = 2$	
$x^2 + y^2 + 3$		$x - y + 9$

Note here again this question involves a straight calculation without apparent shortcut. Notice also that there is a 9 in Column B and a 3 in Column A. Why do you think those particular numbers were chosen by the test-maker? Therefore Choice C would be correct.

One more:

Column A	Column B
Harry bought y crates of oranges of which there are 40 oranges to a crate. He lost 2 crates of oranges and 13 loose oranges. He had 27 oranges left.	
y	3

Here again a straight calculation is involved without apparent shortcut, and you have a number like 3 in one of the columns. Thus Choice C is correct.

NOW BEWARE: If the test-maker is trying to test something other than a calculation or if you know a shortcut, Choice C may <u>not</u> be correct. Here are some examples:

```
Column A                          Column B


     A = (y - 3)(y + 4)
     B = (y - 2)(y + 5)


Value of A when        Value of B when
y = 3                  y = 3
```

Here the test maker is trying to see that if you substitute y = 3, for y in A = (y - 3)(y + 4) you will immediately get A = 0, and when you substitute y = 3 for y in B = (y -2)(y + 5), you will get something <u>positive without having to get the value of B</u>. Since Column A = 0, and Column B is positive, Choice B is correct. So this question involves somewhat of a shortcut and not a straight calculation, so Choice C is not the correct answer.

Another example to watch out for when using the Choice C method:

```
Column A                          Column B


The length of the
hypotenuse of a right                    6
triangle, if the legs
have lengths of 5 and 3
```

Here the test-maker feels that many students would <u>add</u> 5 + 3 in Column A and feel that Column A is greater than Column B. That result is of course incorrect. The hypotenuse, h, is calculated as follows where the legs of the triangle are 5 and 3:

$$h^2 = 5^2 + 3^2 = 25 + 9 = 34$$

So Column A and B become:

Column A	Column B
$\sqrt{34}$	6

Now there is also a shortcut involved. Instead of calculating what $\sqrt{34}$ is and comparing that with 6, let's "square" both columns. We get

Column A	Column B
$\sqrt{34} \times \sqrt{34} = 34$	$6 \times 6 = 36$

And since $34 < 36$,   Choice B is correct.

So, I caution you to be careful when you want to choose Choice C by the preceding methods. Certainly try to work out the problem if there is time. But make sure that if you are going to use the CHOICE C method of guessing that the question involves a straight calculation, with no apparent shortcut and with no other motive of the test-maker for choosing another choice other than Choice C.

PRACTICE
EXERCISES

PRACTICE EXERCISES

The last section of this book contains two chapters of SAT-type problems -- one chapter for verbal problems and one for math problems. They will give you the opportunity to practice the strategies you have learned. Each problem is modeled after a specific SAT question that appeared on a recent exam. The first three reading comprehension passages and associated questions are from actual SAT exams, reprinted with permission of Educational Testing Service, the copyright owner.

Before each problem you will see the number of the strategy in this book that will be useful in solving it.

However, when you work with these problems, try not to look back at the strategies first. See if you can solve each problem without looking back. Look back only if you find you don't know how to approach a problem. It's a good idea to put off starting on these practice problems until you are reasonably sure that you have mastered the strategies.

The discussions after the answers will help you if you find you got an answer wrong. When this happens, work on the problem until you find out where you went wrong. If you don't understand how a particular strategy can be used to solve the problem, work at it until you do understand. Remember, each problem in these two chapters is based on an actual SAT question. If you get a problem wrong, you'll get any similar SAT question wrong too. If you learn where you went wrong, and can handle the problem the next time you see it, you'll add points to your SAT score. Good luck!

PRACTICE YOUR VERBAL STRATEGIES

Antonyms

Below are four antonym questions. In each question, which choice is the opposite of the word in capitals?

1. Strategy No. 10

   DRAWBACK: (A) advantage (B) prescription (C) conclusion (D) disturbance (E) acknowledgement

2. Strategy No. 10

   PERISHABLE: (A) nonexistent (B) inconceivable (C) not likely to spoil (D) not accustomed to routine (E) not likely to forge ahead

3. Strategy No. 11

   STUPEFY: (A) solidify (B) condemn (C) acknowledge (D) liven (E) belittle

4. Strategy No. 11

   FRUITLESS: (A) acidic (B) clever (C) understandable (D) productive (E) carnivorous

Analogies

Questions 5-12 are antonym questions. Of course, in addition to the specific strategy listed before each one, you should use the general Analogy Question strategy of making sentences out of the analogy.

5. Strategy No. 14

   THREAD : BUTTON :: (A) coat : collar (B) shoelace : shoe (C) adhesive : bandaid (D) glue : paste (E) saw : wood

6. Strategy No. 14

   ARMY : GENERAL :: (A) play : director (B) college : professor (C) orchestra : conductor (D) violin : instrument (E) audience : actor

7. Strategy No. 15

   ANVIL : BLACKSMITH :: (A) painting : artist (B) loom : weaver (C) mound : pitcher (D) school : sculptor (E) music : musician

8. Strategy No. 15

   GIRDERS : RIVET:: (A) houses : carpenter (B) bridges : water (C) cement : concrete (D) boards : nail (E) building : foundation

9. Strategy No. 17

   RADIO : EAR :: (A) dial : station (B) music : listen (C) phonograph : loudness (D) silent movie : eye (E) news : attention

10. Strategy No. 17

   FOOD : STARVE :: (A) alcohol : become drunk (B) liquid : boil (C) vitamin : growth (D) air : suffocate (E) protein : deprive

11. Strategy No. 16

CHARLATAN : DECEITFUL :: (A) person who steals : thieving (B) runner : fatigued (C) craftsman : punctual (D) salesman : profitable (E) stethoscope : medical

12. Strategy No. 16

BRAGGART : BOASTFUL :: (A) cautious person : humble (B) criminal : dangerous (C) hater of mankind : misanthropic (D) magician : prophetic (E) saint : religious

Sentence Completion

The next set of questions in the Verbal Section will test your skill in handling sentence completion questions.

13. Strategy No. 18,19

Since we have many cornfields in this city, we do not have to ---- corn.

(A) distribute (B) develop (C) contain (D) import (E) eat

14. Strategy No. 18,19

Unfortunately, many times insurance companies do not insure the person who really may ---- the insurance.

(A) sanctify (B) appall (C) consider (D) reneg (E) need

15. Strategy No. 18,19

I never can tolerate a situation which is ----, in other words, where nothing seems to go anywhere.

(A) abrupt (B) uncomfortable (C) uncontrollable (D) static (E) pliant

16. Strategy No. 20

While a television course is not able to ---- a live course, it is still able to teach the ---- aspects of the subject.

(A) develop...necessary
(B) replace...important
(C) manage...relevant
(D) create...negative
(E) anticipate...inconsequential

17. Strategy No. 20

This is a poem which elicits great ---, unlike many which give the impression of utter ----.

(A) chaos...confusion
(B) understanding...happiness
(C) joy...sorrow
(D) knowledge...intelligence
(E) hatred...solemnity

18. Strategy No. 21

By realizing how much ---- the author had, we can see how he created so many books on different subjects.

(A) intensity (B) knowledge (C) enthusiasm (D) intelligence (E) time

19. Strategy No. 21

Although some ---- the performance, most either thought that it was mediocre or actually disliked it.

(A) enjoyed (B) ignored (C) belittled (D) scrutinized (E) considered

20. Strategy No. 22

If there is no ---- for the product, ---- promotion alone will not convince people to buy it.

(A) precursor...lackadaisical
(B) despondency...superficial
(C) need...extensive
(D) development...stringent
(E) contract...expeditious

21. Strategy No. 22

Dr. Paul's clear and ---- analysis of the subject won her great literary acclaim.

(A) esoteric (B) superficial (C) jaundiced (D) vestigial (E) precise

Reading Comprehension

The remainder of the questions in the Verbal Section will test your skill in handling reading comprehension questions. All use the main reading comprehension strategy: Strategy 23.

A scientific theory is a step--in both senses of the word--toward understanding. A useful theory is in itself an advancement of our knowledge, and it is also a firm base for further advancement. Scientific theories are intellectual constructs that relate broad collections of experimentally observed facts. The advancement of knowledge inherent in a theory is in this relating or "explaining" of otherwise isolated and trivial sets of facts. The base for further advancement is in prediction, guidance of new experiments, and extension to new and broader theories. The basis, existence, and function of a scientific theory are pervaded by experimental observation.

Here, then, is why the atomic theory of the ancients cannot be considered a scientific theory in the modern sense. It was not based on observation, nor did it lead to experiments or further theories. Indeed, the notion of the "ultimate particle" discouraged both experiment and speculation beyond this point. As long as the existence of atoms was postulated only because it seemed fitting, beautiful, moral, or God's will, no science had been created, and no understanding had been approached. But when John Dalton, in 1804, postulated an atomic structure because matter behaves in such a way that it must be particulate, our understanding took a long and bold step forward. The atomic theory became a scientific theory.

22. Which of the following best describes the content of the passage?

(A) A description of the first atomic theory
(B) An explanation of the characteristics of a scientific theory
(C) Advice to students concerning the application of a scientific theory
(D) A summary of events leading to Dalton's theory of atomic structure
(E) A condemnation of present confusion about the nature of scientific theories

23. Which of the following pairs of words best represents what the author means by "both senses" of the word "step" (lines 1-2)?

(A) Space and size
(B) Challenge and rebuttal
(C) Imagination and success
(D) Foundation and progression
(E) Experiment and observation

24. It can be inferred that the ancients' atomic theory was based primarily on

(A) previous scientific theories
(B) primitive scientific experiments
(C) philosophical or theological judgments
(D) observations of isolated facts
(E) attempts to stimulate new experimentation

The land has housed us, clothed us, and fed us, but again and again, out of indifference or sheer stupidity, we have squan-
Line dered resources, defiled, destroyed, and
5 moved on. The land was so rich, so abundant, so very good, we believed, that there was just no end to its capacity to produce or to recover from our mistakes. "There is always more where that came from," we said.
10 Now, however, in the last third of the twentieth century, we are thinking differently. Our waste--our cutting down of entire forests, our poisoning of air and water, our mindless interference with the vital life
15 cycles of plants and animals--is catching up with us. Although our productivity and our prosperity grow steadily, scientists keep warning of the terrible day of reckoning. As any thoughtful person realizes, we Ameri-
20 cans and our land have reached a stage of crisis.
Future historians will no doubt point to this as the time when we first traveled far enough toward the stars to see with our own eyes our earth-home whole: a mere speck in space, but still our only home and the only source of life we know anything about.

25. All of the following are specifically mentioned in the passage as misuses of the Earth's resources EXCEPT

(A) interfering with the life cycle of plants and animals
(B) poisoning the water
(C) squandering our natural resources
(D) destroying our forests
(E) ruining the ecological balance of the oceans

26. In describing American attitudes about the land (lines 7-8), the author implies that

(A) people were shortsighted
(B) people's desires were limited
(C) America's resources were inexhaustible
(D) America has always been short on resources
(E) individuals must look out for their own best interests

27. According to the passage, for which of the following reasons did we exploit the land?

I. Carelessness
II. Insensitivity
III. A desire to conquer the land in order to move the frontier forward

(A) I only (B) I and II only (C) I and III only (D) II and III only (E) I, II, and III

Perhaps it is a kind of ethnic chauvinism that is responsible for the fact that many physiologists and nutritionists were surprised to discover that a large percentage of the human adult population is deficient in lactase, the enzyme that breaks down lactose (milk sugar). The few human populations in which lactose tolerance exceeds intolerance include most Northern European and white American ethnic groups.

A period of active investigation of lactose intolerance was initiated at the end of the 1950's. In 1965 investigators who had administered lactose to American blacks and whites reported some startling findings: whereas only fifteen per cent of the whites showed clinical symptoms of lactose intolerance, about seventy per cent of the blacks were lactose intolerant.

In the study various methods of measuring intolerance were used. One was recording the appearance of clinical symptoms after the ingestion of a dose of lactose, which was standardized at two grams of lactose per kilogram of body weight up to a maximum of 100 grams. Another measured low lactase activity, determined through an intestinal biopsy, after ingestion of the lactose. A third recorded the elevation of blood glucose after ingestion of the lactose.

Since clinical symptoms are variable, and the biopsy method is inconvenient for the subject being tested, the blood-glucose method was preferred. It is a direct measure of lactose breakdown, and false negative results are rare if the glucose is measured fifteen minutes after lactose is administered.

By 1970 enough data had been accumulated to indicate that more people all over the world are intolerant to lactose than are tolerant.

28. On the basis of the information in the passage, which of the following conclusions can be made about the participants in the 1965 study?

(A) The majority of the participants were black.
(B) The majority of the participants were white.
(C) None of the participants exhibited clinical symptoms of lactose intolerance.
(D) A majority of the blacks were intolerant to lactose.
(E) A majority of the whites had a lactase deficiency.

29. The main purpose of the passage is to

(A) report on the use of a new technical procedure
(B) challenge the significance of recent experimental data
(C) describe the investigation of a common condition
(D) analyze the reasons for a medical phenomenon
(E) describe the symptoms of a human ailment

30. According to the passage, a person receiving the maximum dosage of lactose would weigh at least

(A) 10 kilograms
(B) 50 kilograms
(C) 100 kilograms
(D) 150 kilograms
(E) 200 kilograms

31. The author suggests that prior to the late 1950's, scientists were unaware of the common occurrence of lactose intolerance in adults because

(A) lactose intolerance was not prevalent among white ethnic groups
(B) they did not know the symptoms of lactose intolerance
(C) they had not identified the function of lactase in human digestion
(D) they did not know the source of lactose in the human diet
(E) it was not yet possible to measure enzyme activities

Mist continues to obscure the horizon, but above us the sky is suddenly awash with lavender light. At once the geese respond.
Line Now, as well as their cries, a beating roar
5 rolls across the water as if five thousand housewives have taken it into their heads to shake out blankets all at one time. Ten thousand housewives. It keeps up--the invisible rhythmic beating of all those goose
10 wings--for what seems a long time. Even Lonnie is held motionless with suspense.
Then the geese begin to rise. One, two, three hundred--then a thousand at a time-- in long horizontal lines that unfurl like
15 pennants across the sky. The horizon actually darkens as they pass. It goes on and on like that, flock after flock, for three or four minutes, each new contingent announcing its ascent with an accel-
20 erating roar of cries and wingbeats. Then gradually the intervals between flights became longer. I think the spectacle is over, until yet another flock lifts up, following the others in a gradual turn
25 toward the northeastern quadrant of the refuge.
Finally the sun emerges from the mist; the mist itself thins a little, uncovering the black line of willows on the
30 other side of the wildlife preserve. I remember to close my mouth--which has been open for some time--and inadvertently shut two or three mosquitoes inside. Only a few

straggling geese oar their way across the
35 sun's red surface. Lonnie wears an exasper-
ated, proprietary expression, as if he had
produced and directed the show himself and
had just received a bad review. "It would
have been better with more light," he says;
40 "I can't always guarantee just when they'll
start moving." I assure him I thought it
was a fantastic sight. "Well," he rumbles,
"I guess it wasn't too bad."

32. In the descriptive phrase, "shake out
blankets all at one time" (line 7), the
author is appealing chiefly to the
reader's

(A) background
(B) sight
(C) emotions
(D) thoughts
(E) hearing

33. The mood created by the author is one of

(A) tranquility
(B) excitement
(C) sadness
(D) bewilderment
(E) unconcern

34. The main idea expressed by the author
about the geese is that they

(A) are spectacular to watch
(B) are unpredictable
(C) disturb the environment
(D) produce a lot of noise
(E) fly in large flocks

35. Judging from the passage, the reader
can conclude that

(A) the speaker dislikes nature's
inconveniences
(B) the geese's timing is predictable
(C) Lonnie has had the experience before
(D) both observers are hunters
(E) the author and Lonnie are the same
person

        Those who save money are often accused
of loving money; but, in my opinion, those
who love money most are those who spend it.
Line To them money is not merely a list of dead
5 figures in a bankbook. It is an animate
thing, spasmodically restless like the birds
in a wood, taking wings to itself, as the
poet has said. Money, to the man who enjoys
spending, is the perfect companion--a com-
10 panion all the dearer because it never out-
stays its welcome. It is responsive to his
every mood.... Age, alas, has blotted out
half that world of passionate delight in
which I once lived, and to many of the
15 things I once loved I have grown indiffer-
ent. The love of money, however, remains.
So much do I love it that I feel almost a
different person when I have money in my
pocket and when I have none. Let me have
20 but money, and, for the time being, I am
back among the ardent attachments and illusions of the nursery.

From all this I am inclined to conclude
that the love of money is a form of infant-
25 ilism. The man who loves money is the man who
has never grown up. He has never passed from
the world of fairy tales into the world of
philosophy (for philosophy, which is the
wisdom of the grown man in contrast to the
30 wonder of the child, is as contemptuous of
money as it is of jam, sweets, and bubble
gum). Money, according to the philosophers,
is dross, filthy lucre, an impediment rather
than an aid to true happiness. Those who re-
35 tain the nursery imagination throughout life,
however, cannot be persuaded of this. Money
they regard as the loveliest gift ever be-
stowed on a mortal by the wand of a fairy
godmother. They are like boys dreaming of a
40 Treasure Island; and their money-bags become almost as dear to them as--sometimes,
dearer than--their country.

36. According to the first paragraph, money
has the quality of

(A) changing a personality
(B) causing restlessness
(C) outstaying its welcome
(D) inspiring greed
(E) retaining the memories of childhood

37. During the author's lifetime, many things
have changed for him except his

(A) interest in sports
(B) fear of old age
(C) contempt for philosophy
(D) desire to return to his childhood
(E) love of money

38. Which expression in the second paragraph describes the characteristics of
men who like money?

(A) "I am inclined to conclude" (line 23)
(B) "the wisdom of the grown man" (line 29)
(C) "contemptuous of money" (lines 30-31)
(D) "Money is dross, filthy lucre"
(lines 32-33)
(E) "like boys dreaming of a Treasure
Island" (lines 39-40)

39. The author implies that the "ardent attachments and illusions of the nursery"
(lines 21-22) include

(A) bankbooks and checkbooks
(B) animals and birds
(C) jams, sweets, and bubble gum
(D) parents and companions
(E) dross and lucre

The theatre is a jungle in which the playwright, the actor, and the director struggle for supremacy. Sometimes the fight goes one way and then, for a time, another. I have lived through the reign of each in turn and now it seems to me the playwright is once more supreme. Pinter, Stoppard, and Gray stalk unchallenged by Olivier and Peter Brook. Once more the audience is invited not only to look and listen but to think as they once thought with Shaw and Galsworthy. There is a rich heritage in the British theatre, but it is not, alas, the heritage of the actor, still less of the director. The playwright must in the final battle always prove the winner. His work, imperishable; his fame, enduring. I write "alas" because although I have tried my hand at both directing and playwrighting, I am in essence one of those of whom Shakespeare wrote that we were destined to strut and fret an hour upon the stage and then be heard no more.

My generation of actors were trained to entice our prey. We kept an eye open, a claw sharpened, even when we professed to slumber. However deep the tragedy or shallow the farce, we never forgot to face front. Nowadays, the relation between player and public tends to be more sophisticated. Together they share a mutual experience of pain and sorrow. Sometimes the actor seems able to dispense with his audience--to no longer need them. He may choose or chance to perfect his performances on a wet afternoon in Shewsbury, with hardly anyone watching, and thereafter the repetition for him may stale. For me this never happens. I never perfect a performance, though obviously I am sometimes better or worse, but I have learned that without a perfect audience, my struggle to the summit is impossible. I am aware as the curtain rises of the texture of the house.

40. According to the passage, Pinter, Stoppard, and Gray are involved with the theatre as

(A) theatre owners
(B) actors
(C) playwrights
(D) directors
(E) investors

41. The author believes that the audience

(A) is vital
(B) is a necessary evil
(C) is largely irrelevant
(D) would rather not think
(E) prefers comedy to tragedy

42. According to the passage, what is the author's usual occupation in the theater?

(A) playwright
(B) director
(C) reviewer
(D) producer
(E) actor

Many archeologists assume that Ice Age animal images represent only a form of hunting magic. The hunter, so the theory runs, made an animal image and "killed" it, then went out and hunted with the power of magic on his side. Still other archeologists theorize that the animals were totems— figures of ancestor animals from which different human groups or clans supposedly descended. The animals have also been interpreted as sexual symbols, with certain species representing the male principle and others the female. I was now to ask new questions.

When I put the Vogelherd horse under the microcope, I discovered that its ear, nose, mouth and eye had been carefully and accurately carved, but that these features had been worn down by long handling. The figure had obviously been kept by its owner and used for a considerable period. Clearly it had not been created for the purpose of being "killed" at once.

But in the shoulder of the horse was engraved one unworn angle that I took to represent a dart or wound. Apparently some time late in the use of this figure, it had been killed. But why? Was the killing intended as hunting magic? Perhaps. But if Cro-Magnon was as sophisticated as I was beginning to find he was, could the killing not have been for some other symbolic purpose, such as initiation, the casting of a spell. the curing of illness, a sacrifice for the coming of winter, or the celebration for the coming spring?

Whatever the meaning, here was an indication that Ice Age images, like notations and certain tools, were made to be kept and used over a long period for specific purposes.

43. In line 7, the dash is used to

(A) take the place of a semicolon
(B) set off a definition
(C) introduce a list
(D) indicate that something has been left out
(E) offer relatively unimportant information

44. What does the passage imply about the author?

(A) He is not familiar with Cro-Magnon man's hunting strategies
(B) He has personally examined numerous Ice Age artifacts
(C) He has found new evidence about Cro-Magnon man from recent diggings
(D) He has known about the significance of the Vogelherd horse for a long time
(E) He was the first scientist to learn of the existence of the Vogelherd horse

45. Which sentence best summarizes the main idea of this passage?

(A) "Many archeologists assume that Ice Age animal images represent only a form of hunting magic." (lines 1 through 3)
(B) "I was now to ask new questions" (lines 13 and 14)
(C) "Clearly it had not been created for the purpose of being 'killed' at once." (lines 22 and 23)
(D) "But in the shoulder of the horse was engraved one unknown angle that I took to represent a dart or wound." (lines 24 through 26)
(E) "Whatever the meaning, here was an indication that Ice Age images, like notations and certain tools, were made to be kept over a long period or for specific purposes." (lines 37 through 41)

46. The overall tone of this passage may be described as

(A) argumentative
(B) suspended
(C) questioning
(D) humorous
(E) resentful

It was at Arles, the small city in the south of France where he stayed from early 1888 to the spring of 1889, that Vincent van Gogh had his first real bout with madness. After a quarrel with Paul Gauguin, he cut off part of his own ear. Yet Arles was also the scene of an astonishing burst of creativity. Over the short span of 15 months, van Gogh produced some 200 paintings and more than 100 drawings and watercolors, a record that only Picasso has matched in the modern era. Orchards and wheatfields under the glowing sun, neighbors and townspeople, interiors of the Yellow House where he lived, were all subjects of his frenetic brush. The Arles canvases, alive with color--vermillion, emerald green, Prussian blue and a particularly brilliant yellow--have intensity of feeling that mark the high point of his career, and deeply affected the work of artists to follow, notably the Fauves and the German Expressionists.

Van Gogh went to Arles after two years in Paris, where his beloved younger brother Theo, who supported him psychologically and financially for most of his adult life, was an art dealer. In Paris, Vincent had met Gauguin, and other important artists--Lautrec, Degas, Pissarro, and Seurat. Like the last two, he worked in the Neo-Impressionist or Pointillist style--applying color in tiny dots or strokes that "mixed" in the viewer's eye to create effects of considerable intensity. But he wanted "gayer" colors than Paris provided, the kind of atmoshere evoked by the Japanese prints he so admired. Then, too, the French capital had exhausted him, mentally and physically. He felt that in Arles, not exactly a bustling arts center, he might find serenity, and even establish an artistic tradition.

It was van Gogh's hope of founding a new artists' colony in the south that made him eager to have Gauguin, whose talent van Gogh readily recognized, join him at Arles. The plan, on Vincent's part, was for Gauguin to stay in Arles for maybe a year, working and sharing with him the small living quarters and studio he had found for himself and dubbed the Yellow House. At first, the two men got along well. But they did not at all agree on judgments of other artists. Still, Gauguin had an influence on van Gogh. Gauguin began pushing the younger artist to paint from memory rather than actuality.

Before the year was up, whether because of Gauguin's attempts to change van Gogh's style, or what, the two men had apparently begun to get on each other's nerves. Gauguin wrote to Theo that he felt he had to return to Paris, citing his and Vincent's "temperamental incompatibility." A letter from Vincent to Theo followed, noting that Gauguin was "a little out of sorts with the good town of Arles, and especially with me."

But then, the two apparently made up-- but not for long. Gauguin returned to Paris and never saw van Gogh again, although they later had friendly correspondence.

47. Which of the following is the best title for the passage?

(A) Where Van Gogh's Art Reached Its Zenith
(B) An Unfortunate Mismatch Between Two Great Artists
(C) Another Tale of a Genius Unable to Adjust to Society
(D) A Prolific Painter Whose Art Will Live On
(E) Van Gogh's Frustration in His Hope to Found a New Artists' Colony

48. According to the passage, which of the following statements is not true?

(A) Fauvism is a movement in painting typified by vivid colors.
(B) Gauguin was an older man than Theo.
(C) Pissarro was a painter associated with the Neo-Impressionist school.
(D) Van Gogh's work began to deteriorate after Gauguin's departure from Arles.
(E) Van Gogh's behavior was, at times, quite abnormal.

49. For which of the following reasons did van Gogh decide to leave Paris and go to Arles?

I. He sought a different environment for the kind of painting he wished to do.
II. He had hopes of forming a new artists' colony.
III. He wanted a more peaceful location where there was less stress.

(A) II only
(B) III only
(C) I and II only
(D) I and III only
(E) I, II, and III

50. Gauguin's attitude toward van Gogh is best described in the passage as one of

(A) gentle ridicule
(B) unallayed suspicion
(C) tolerant acceptance
(D) open condescension
(E) resentful admiration

51. Aside from his quarrel with Gauguin, we may infer that a major contributory reason for van Gogh's going to the extreme of cutting off part of his ear was his

(A) concern about being able to support himself financially
(B) inability to get along with Gauguin
(C) failure to form an artists' colony in Arles
(D) mental and emotional instability
(E) being upset by Gauguin's attempts to change his style

As in the case of so many words used by the biologist and physiologist, the word acclimatization is hard to define. With increase in knowledge and understanding, meanings of words change. Originally the term acclimatization was taken to mean only the ability of human beings or animals or plants to accustom themselves to new and strange climatic conditions, primarily altered temperature. A person or a wolf moves to a hot climate and is uncomfortable there, but after a time is better able to withstand the heat. But aside from temperature, there are other aspects of climate. A person or an animal may become adjusted to living at higher altitudes than those it was originally accustomed to. At really high altitudes, such as aviators might be exposed to, the low atmospheric pressure becomes a factor of primary importance. In changing to a new environment, a person may, therefore, meet new conditions of temperature or pressure, and in addition may have to contend with different chemical surroundings. On high mountains, the amount of oxygen in the atmosphere may be relatively small; in crowded cities, a person may become exposed to relatively high concentrations of carbon dioxide or even carbon monoxide, and in various areas may be exposed to conditions in which the water content of the atmosphere is extremely high or extremely low. Thus in the case of humans, animals, and even plants, the concept of acclimatization includes the phenomena of increased toleration of high or low temperature, of altered pressure and of changes in the chemical environment.

Let us define acclimatization, therefore, as the process in which an organism or a part of an organism becomes accustomed or inured to an environment which is normally unsuitable to it or lethal for it. By and large, acclimatization is a relatively slow process. The term should not be taken to include relatively rapid adjustments such as our sense organs are constantly making. This type of adjustment is commonly referred to by physiologists as "adaptation." Thus our touch sense soon becomes accustomed to the pressure of our clothes and we do not feel them; we soon fail to hear the ticking of a clock; obnoxious odors after a time fail to make much impression on us, and our eyes in strong light rapidly become insensitive.

The fundamental fact about acclimatization is that all animals and plants have some capacity to adjust themselves to changes in their environment. This is one of the most remarkable characteristics of living organisms, a characteristic for which it is extremely difficult to find explanations.

52. According to the reading selection, all animals and plants

(A) have an ability for acclimatization.
(B) can adjust to only one change in the environment at a time.
(C) are successful in adjusting themselves to changes in their environments.
(D) can adjust to natural changes in the environment but not to artificially induced changes.
(E) that have once acclimatized themselves to an environmental change can acclimatize themselves more rapidly to subsequent changes.

53. It can be inferred from the reading selection that

(A) every change in the environment requires acclimatization by living things.
(B) plants and animals are more alike than they are different.
(C) biologists and physiologists study essentially the same things.
(D) the explanation of acclimatization is specific to each plant and animal.
(E) as science develops the connotation of terms may change.

54. According to the reading selection, acclimatization

(A) is similar to adaptation.
(B) is more important today than formerly.
(C) involves positive as well as negative adjustment.
(D) may be involved with a part of an organism but not with the whole organism.
(E) is more difficult to explain with the more complex present-day environment than formerly.

55. By inference from the reading selection, which one of the following would not require the process of acclimatization?

(A) An ocean fish placed in a lake
(B) A skin diver making a deep dive
(C) An airplane pilot making a high-altitude flight
(D) A person going from daylight into a darkened room
(E) A businessman moving from Denver, Colorado to New Orleans, Louisiana

56. According to the passage, a major dis-
tiction between acclimatization and
adaptation is that acclimatization

(A) is more important than adaptation
(B) is relatively slow and adaptation is
relatively rapid
(C) applies to adjustments while adaptation does not apply to adjustments
(D) applies to terrestrial animals and
adaptation to aquatic animals
(E) is applicable to all animals and
plants and adaptation only to
higher animals and man

Answers to Antonym Questions

1. A. DRAWBACK is a negative (-) word. Look for positive (+) words in choices: (A) advantage is +, (B) prescription is neutral (O), (C) conclusion is O, (D) disturbance is -, (E) acknowledgement is O. The only positive word is (A) advantage.

2. C. PERISHABLE is a negative word. Look for positive words: (A) nonexistent is -, (B) inconceivable is -, (C) not likely to spoil is + because it contains two negatives, not and spoil, and two negatives make a positive. (D) not accustomed to routine is -, (E) not likely to forge ahead is -.

3. D. Listen to the sound of the word: STUPEFY is related to the word stupor and means "to put in a stupor." (Don't confuse it with the word stupid!) Its opposite is (D) liven.

4. D. FRUITLESS means "bearing no fruit." Its opposite is productive. Watch for traps like acidic. Strategy No. 10 would also help with this question.

Answers to Analogy Questions

5. C. A thread is used to hold a button in place, as adhesive is used to hold a bandaid in place. Look out for traps like shoelace: shoe. (A shoelace ties up a shoe, but doesn't hold it permanently in place for the length of its useful life.)

6. C. An army is a body of men commanded by a general; an orchestra is a body commanded by a conductor. Look out for traps like Choice A. A play is, in a sense, commanded by a director, but it is not a group of people. If the analogy had been actors: director or players: director, it would have been more nearly correct.

7. B. Use reverse order. Say "A blacksmith does his work on an anvil the way a . . . weaver does work on a loom."

8. D. Again, reverse order. "Rivets hold girders together . . . Nails hold boards together."

9. D. Radio is perceived by the ear the way a silent movie is perceived by the eye. Beware of choices like phonograph: loudness, which also deal with sound, but whose elements are not related the way radio: ear is.

10. D. Lack of food causes us to starve, lack of air causes us to suffocate. Again, look out for superficial relationships like alcohol: drunk or vitamin: growth.

11. A. When you see a noun-adjective pair, chances are that they are either synonymous or opposites. In the choices, there are no opposites, and only the choices of (A) mean the same things. You could get the right answer even if you didn't know that a CHARLATAN is a faker, a deceitful person.

12. C. Here the choices BRAGGART and BOASTFUL mean the same thing. The choices narrow down to B and to C (a possibility if you don't know what misanthrope means). A criminal may not always be dangerous--for example, a bank clerk who steals money is not dangerous. Misanthropic means "being a hater of mankind" just as BOASTFUL means "being a BRAGGART."

Answers to Sentence Completion Questions

13. D. Key words: since, have. We don't have to import corn since we have cornfields.

14. E. Key words: unfortunately, really

15. D. Key words: in other words. Translate the words following the key-word phrase: "where nothing seems to go anywhere" into the word static.

16. B. Use the positive-negative approach. Key words: while (meaning "although"), still. The key words tell you that the two clauses of the sentence are being contrasted. The first clause is negative, with a not in it. The second clause must therefore be positive. Choice B makes the best sense with this construction.

17. C. Also a sentence with two contrasting parts, as shown by the key word unlike. Choice C, with two words that are antonyms, fits the bill.

147

18. B. Work backwards from the second part of the sentence. The key words we can see that . . . show that the second part of the sentence must follow logically from the first. Since the author created books on many different subjects, he must have had a lot of knowledge.

19. A. Again, work backwards. Key words: although, most, mediocre, disliked. If most people disliked the performance, the obvious contrast is that some enjoyed it.

20. C. Don't be scared or led astray by difficult words in choices, like lackadaisical, stringent, and expeditious. They may not be correct. The sentence seeems to make most sense using the easy words need and extensive.

21. E. Again, don't be scared by difficult words like esoteric, jaundiced, vestigial. Precise is correct (since the missing word is joined by and to the word clear, the word is probably a near-synonym of clear). Precise fits the bill.

Answers to Reading Comprehension Questions

22. B	32. E	42. E	52. A
23. D	33. B	43. B	53. E
24. C	34. A	44. B	54. A
25. E	35. C	45. E	55. D
26. A	36. A	46. C	56. B
27. B	37. E	47. A	
28. D	38. E	48. D	
29. C	39. C	49. E	
30. B	40. C	50. C	
31. A	41. A	51. D	

PRACTICE YOUR MATH STRATEGIES

Regular Math

Problems 1 - 11 will give you practice in using two very important math strategies: working backward from Choice E when you must test all choices, and using the "translation technique" in rendering verbal problems into mathematical form. Both strategies require you to analyze the problem before you actually start working on it. So, as you look at each problem, make sure you understand why its particular strategy applies.

1. Strategy No. 35

   When you divide a number by 1/3 you get the same result as if you multiplied that number by

   (A) 1/3 (B) 0.3 (C) 6 (D) $33\frac{1}{3}$% (E) 3

2. Strategy No. 35

   Of the following, which number is odd?

   (A) 6 X 7 (B) 71 - 17 (C) 57 + 27
   (D) 75 ÷ 5 (E) 4^3

3. Strategy No. 35

   The ratio of two whole numbers is NOT equal to which of the following?

   (A) 1/5 (B) 0.5 (C) 5% (D) 5^2/2 (E) $\sqrt{5}$/1

4. Strategy No. 35

   Which of the following pairs of numbers are UNEQUAL?

   (A) $\frac{1}{125}$, 0.008 (B) 4.3, $\frac{43}{10}$ (C) $\frac{5}{7}$, $\frac{55}{77}$
   (D) $\frac{18}{96}$, $\frac{3}{16}$ (E) $\frac{68}{16}$, $\frac{32}{6}$

5. Strategy No. 35

   x is a number less than 0. Which of the following must be true?

   (A) 2 ÷ 2 = x (B) x ÷ 2 = 2 (C) 2 ÷ x = x
   (D) x ÷ x = x (E) x ÷ x = 1

6. Strategy No. 35

   If $x(\frac{2}{y})$ = 2, which is not always true?

   (A) $xy = x^2$ (B) x-y = 0 (C) $x^2 + y^2 = 2y^2$
   (D) x + y = 2y (E) $x = \frac{1}{y}$

7. Strategy No. 36

   Mr. Harris is P years old. He is also 4 years older than Mrs. Jones. How many years old was Mrs. Jones 3 years ago?

   (A) P - 7 (B) P - 1 (C) P + 1
   (D) P + 7 (E) P - 4

8. Strategy No. 36

   Harry and Paul were playing a certain card game. Harry scored 35% more points than Paul scored. If Paul scored 60 points, what was Harry's score?

   (A) 60 (B) 70 (C) 65 (D) 81 (E) 92

9. Strategy No. 36

   If p is divided by q and this result is then subtracted from the sum of p and q, the final result is

   (A) q/p - (p+q) (B) p/q - (p+q)
   (C) (p+q) - p/q (D) (p+q) - q/p (E) 1

10. Strategy No. 36 _____

Cindy is three times as old as Jeffrey. Two years ago, she was 4 times as old as Jeffrey was then. What is Jeffrey's age now?

(A) 4 (B) 5 (C) 6 (D) 7 (E) 8

11. Strategy No. 36,37 _____

3/5 of the people at a party are married and 2/3 of the married are over 30 years of age. What fraction of the people at the party are married who are under or equal to 30 years of age?

(A) $\frac{6}{15}$ (B) $\frac{3}{5}$ (C) $\frac{2}{3}$ (D) $\frac{1}{5}$ (E) Cannot be determined

The next pair of problems also illustrates an important analytical strategy: looking for the part of the problem that gives you the most information before you actually start working on it.

12. Strategy No. 38 _____

If a/2 is an even integer and a/4 is an odd integer, then it is possible that a could equal

(A) 104 (B) 14 (C) 44 (D) 88 (E) 16

13. Strategy No. 38 _____

If m ranges in value from 0.01 to 0.1 and n ranges in value from 1.0 to 100.0, then the minimum value of m/n is

(A) 0.0001 (B) 0.001 (C) 0.01 (D) 0.1 (E) 1.0

Here are a group of problems that have in common the strategy of finding an unknown area or length by subtraction from a known quantity or length.

14. Strategy No. 39 _____

In the above figure, the larger circle has radius a and the smaller circle has diameter a. What is the area of the region that is shaded?

(A) πa^2 (B) 0 (C) $\frac{3\pi a^2}{4}$ (D) $\frac{\pi a^2}{4}$ (E) $\frac{1}{2}\pi a^2$

15. Strategy No. 39 _____

The area of the unshaded region in the figure below in terms of a, b, and c is

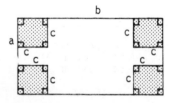

(A) $ba-8c^2$ (B) $4c-ba$ (C) $ba-4c^2$
(D) $ba+4c^2$ (E) ba

16. Strategy No. 39

In the above figure, the center of the circle is O, angle COD = 90°, and side CD of triangle COD is $4\sqrt{2}$. What is the area of the shaded region?

(A) $4\pi - 8$ (B) $4\pi + 8$ (C) 16π (D) $32\pi - 16$
(E) This cannot be determined from the information given.

17. Strategy No. 39

The sides of the square above are divided into three equal segments. The area of the shaded region is A and the area of the square is B. What is the ratio A/B?

(A) $\frac{1}{3}$ (B) $\frac{2}{3}$ (C) $\frac{3}{4}$ (D) $\frac{7}{16}$ (E) $\frac{5}{8}$

The grouping of problems that comes next utilizes a couple of strategies, but the problems themselves have one thing in common: they were designed by the test makers to fool you. Read them carefully, and don't be fooled!

18. Strategy No. 34

A car travels K kilometers in h hours and m minutes. What is the car's average speed in kilometers per hour?

(A) $\frac{K}{h+m}$ (B) $\frac{K+m}{h}$ (C) $(h+\frac{m}{60})K$ (D) $\frac{h+\frac{m}{60}}{K}$

(E) $\frac{K}{h+\frac{m}{60}}$

19. Strategy No. 34

A space shuttle travels at an average rate of 150 miles every x seconds. How many minutes will it take the rocket to travel 3000 miles?

(A) $\frac{3}{x}$ (B) $\frac{x}{3}$ (C) 200x (D) $\frac{200}{x}$ (E) $\frac{x}{200}$

20. Strategy No. 40

What is the average rate in miles per hour of a car going uphill at a rate of 20 mph and downhill the same distance at 30 mph?

(A) 25 (B) 28 (C) 21 (D) 23 (E) 24

21. Strategy No. 41

Test scores of 12 students have an average of 70. When the three highest and the three lowest scores are not computed in the average, the new average becomes 64. The average of the scores eliminated is

(A) 76 (B) 77 (C) 78 (D) 79
(E) impossible to determine.

22. Strategy No. 41

20 students averaged $\underline{t}$ on a test. Test scores ranged form 0 to 100 inclusive. The average score for the first 15 papers graded was 70. What is the difference between the greatest and least possible values of $\underline{t}$?

(A) 20 (B) 25 (C) 30 (D) 35 (E) 40

23. Strategy No. 41

A weekly test had a range in scores from 0 to 100. John got a score of 60 on the first test and 70 on the second test. What is the lowest score John can get on the next test to average 70 on the first five tests?

(A) 20 (B) 40 (C) 50 (D) 60 (E) 70

24. Strategy No. 43

If $(y + \frac{1}{y}) = 9$ then $y^2 + \frac{1}{y^2} = $

(A) 76 (B) 77 (C) 78 (D) 79 (E) 81

25. Strategy No. 43

If $a + b = c$ and $a - b = \frac{2}{c}$ $(c \neq 0)$, then $a^2 - b^2 =$

(A) 2c (B) $\frac{c^2 - 2}{c}$ (C) 1 (D) 2 (E) $\frac{1}{4}$

26. Strategy No. 43

If 4m - n = 9 and 2m - 3n = 5, then m + n =

(A) 2 (B) 4 (C) $\frac{5}{9}$ (D) -4 (E) -2

27. Strategy No. 43

If 7a+4b = 21 and 2a+2b = 9, then $\frac{9a+6b}{15}$ =

(A) 1 (B) 2 (C) 18 (D) 7 (E) 9

Now try a group of problems whose solution involves factoring. (You may also wish to look back at the material involving exponents in the section titled "Arm Yourself" in the Math Prep chapter.)

28. Strategy No. 42

What is the minimum value of $\frac{a + b}{ab}$ if $1 \leqq a < b \leqq 12$ and a and b are integers?

(A) $\frac{13}{12}$ (B) 1 (C) $\frac{23}{132}$ (D) $\frac{39}{135}$ (E) $\frac{24}{144}$

29. Strategy No. 44,42

If 30 X 4000 = 12 X 10^x, x =

(A) 3 (B) 4 (C) 5 (D) 6 (E) 7

30. Strategy No. 44,42

If $(2^6)(5^7) = 5(10^p)$, p =

(A) 4 (B) 5 (C) 6 (D) 7 (E) 8

31. Strategy No. 44

$(3^4 - 3^5)(3^2 - 3) =$

(A) 186 (B) -3^3 X 15 (C) -3^2 X 120 (D) -3^4 X 12 (E) -3^4 X 15

Here's a set of problems that deal with the use of arbitrary symbols:

32. Strategy No. 45

If $\boxed{m} \!-\! \boxed{n} \!-\! \boxed{q} = \frac{mn}{q}$ for all nonzero real numbers of m, n, and q then $\boxed{\frac{1}{4}} \!-\! \boxed{\frac{1}{3}} \!-\! \boxed{\frac{1}{15}} =$

(A) $\frac{4}{5}$ (B) $\frac{1}{12}$ X $\frac{1}{15}$ (C) $\frac{5}{4}$ (D) $\frac{5}{9}$ (E) $\frac{9}{5}$

33. Strategy No. 45

For all real numbers where a ≠ 0, b ≠ 0, c ≠ 0

$(m,p,z ⊕ a,b,c) = \frac{m}{a} + \frac{p}{b} + \frac{z}{c}$

then $(1,2,3 ⊕ -1,-2,-3)$ X $(1,4,1 ⊕ 1,2,1) =$

(A) -6 (B) +6 (C) -12 (D) +12 (E) none of these

34. Strategy No. 45

Where a and b are real and where a ≠ 0 and b ≠ 0 and a ≠ b , the following definition applies:

$$\begin{matrix} a \\ \emptyset \\ b \end{matrix} = \frac{a + b}{a - b}$$

Which of the following is necessarily true?

I. $\begin{matrix} a^2 \\ \emptyset \\ b^2 \end{matrix} = \frac{a^2 + b^2}{a^2 - b^2}$

II. $\begin{matrix} a \\ \emptyset \\ b \end{matrix} = - \begin{matrix} b \\ \emptyset \\ a \end{matrix}$

III. $\begin{matrix} \frac{1}{a} \\ \emptyset \\ \frac{1}{b} \end{matrix} = - \begin{matrix} a \\ \emptyset \\ b \end{matrix}$

(A) I only (B) II only (C) III only
(D) II and III only (E) I, II, III

Each of the last pair of questions contains some unnecessary information. See if you can spot the unnecessary information in each question and can solve the problem without using it.

35. Strategy No. 46

Given the following relations, which of the choices is equal to a?

Relations: $b = \dfrac{2}{5} c$

$f = \dfrac{2}{3} b$

$c = \dfrac{d}{4}$

$d = 3e$

$c = \dfrac{3}{4} a$

(A) b (B) c (C) d (D) e (E) f

36. Strategy No. 48

If 3/4 the area of an equilateral triangle is 12, what is the area of the triangle?

(A) 16 (B) 12 (C) 9 (D) 6 (E) 20

Quantitative Comparisons

Many quantitative comparison questions are solved by canceling quantities from both columns or by eliminating some complicating expression like a square root. The following group of questions will give you practice in using these techniques.

Column A	Column B
1. Strategy No. 54	

The three lines above intersect at a point.

Column A	Column B
a + b	a + c

2. Strategy No. 54

Column A	Column B
$54^2 + (7)(9)(81) + 7^3$	$54^2 - (7)(9)(81) + 7^3$

3. Strategy No. 54

Column A	Column B
m^2	$1 + m^2$

4. Strategy No. 55

Column A	Column B
$\sqrt{6} + \sqrt{13}$	$\sqrt{19}$

5. Strategy No. 55

Column A	Column B
$\sqrt{0.005}$	0.05

6. Strategy No. 54,60

$$3x + 2 = n$$

Column A	Column B
60x + 20	20n

7. Strategy No. 54

Column A	Column B
$\dfrac{2176}{31}$	$\dfrac{2176}{62}$

8. Strategy No. 54

Column A	Column B
5.0 X 7,968	4.9 X 7,968

Here's a small group of problems that can be solved by the use of a variety of rather easy strategies. On some, you may have to operate on the Given or change the quantities to match the Given more closely.

	Column A	Column B		Column A	Column B

9. Strategy No. 56

| 0 | $1 - x$ |

10. Strategy No. 56

$$0 > a > b$$

| a | $-3b$ |

11. Strategy No. 57

| 0.2×0.2 | $\dfrac{1}{400} + \dfrac{1}{400}$ |

12. Strategy No. 57,60

$$bd + cd > a \qquad b + c > 0$$

| $\dfrac{a}{b + c}$ | d |

13. Strategy No. 60,36

$$\text{a percent of b is c}$$
$$c \neq 0$$

| ab/c | 100 |

14. Strategy No. 51,36,60

$$13\% \text{ of } 2x = 120$$

| $13\% \text{ of } x$ | 60 |

In all but one of the following comparisons, you should suspect that the correct answer may be Choice D. As you examine each problem, try to understand why D is such a distinct possibility. Then use the applicable strategies to confirm or eliminate your suspicion. Finally, see if you can spot the one problem where D is not such a distinct possibility -- and can tell why.

	Column A	Column B		Column A	Column B

15. Strategy No. 59 or 58

$$x < 6$$
$$4y < 9$$

| x | y |

16. Strategy No. 59 or 58

$$a > -4$$
$$b < 4$$

| a | b |

17. Strategy No. 59 or 58

$$a^2 - b^2 = 0$$

| a | b |

18. Strategy No. 59 or 51

$$b > 1$$
$$a < 0$$

| $\dfrac{a}{b}$ | ab |

154

Column A	Column B	Column A	Column B

19. Strategy No. 59

$$m > 0$$

Column A	Column B
$m^3 + 2$	$m^4 - 2$

20. Strategy No. 59

$$abc > 0$$
$$a < 0$$

Column A	Column B
b	c

21. Strategy No. 58

Column A	Column B
$m^2 n^4$	$n^2 m^4$

22. Strategy No. 58

$$a > 0$$

Column A	Column B
$(a - 4)(a + 7)$	$(a - 4)^2$

23. Strategy No. 58

$$a > 0, \ b > 0, \ ab = 3$$

Column A	Column B
$a + b$	4

24. Strategy No. 58

a,b,c are all integers greater than 0

Column A	Column B
abc	$a + b + c$

25. Strategy No. 59

$$4x < 12, \ 5y < 10$$
$$x \neq y$$

Column A	Column B
x	y

26. Strategy No. 59

$$-1 < m < +1$$
$$m \neq 0$$

Column A	Column B
m	$\frac{1}{m}$

The reason for grouping this last set of problems together I leave you to figure out. There is one important strategy that covers them all. Try to figure it out without looking it up!

Column A	Column B	Column A	Column B

27. Strategy No. 64,45

ⓧ represents the value of x^3 rounded to nearest integer.

Column A	Column B
The product of ② and 3	④ - 40

28. Strategy No. 64

Sam purchased y oranges and paid 10¢ each for 4 of them and 20¢ each for the rest of the oranges.

Column A	Column B
$40 + 20(y - 4)$	The cost, in cents, of y oranges

29. Strategy No. 64

Shipping Rates for 1 lb. package:

From a to –	First 100 miles	Each additional 100 miles
b	$2.20	$1.70
c	$3.20	$2.00

Column A	Column B
The cost of shipping a 1 lb. package 900 miles from a to c	$19.20

30. Strategy No. 64

$$\frac{1}{3} \quad \frac{1}{7} \quad \frac{3}{4} \quad \frac{2}{3} \quad \frac{5}{8}$$

Column A	Column B
The product of the greatest fraction above and 4/21	The least fraction shown above

155

Column A	Column B		Column A	Column B

31. Strategy No. 64

$$2 + a = b$$

The average of 6, 5, and a	The average of 7, 2, and b

32. Strategy No. 64

A jacket that listed for $45.90 was sold at a 40% discount.

$27.54	Price of jacket after discount

Answers to Regular Math Questions

1-6. In testing choices (Questions 1-6), always work from Choice E backwards.

1. E
2. D
3. E
4. E
5. E
6. E

7. A. Translate: P = 4 + J; P - 4 = J; P - 7 = J - 3.

8. D. Translate: H = (35/100)P + P; H = (35/100)60 + 60; H = 21 + 60 = 81

9. C. Translate: If p is divided by q→p/q; the sum of p and q→p + q; subtracted→-. So answer is p + q - p/q.

10. C. Translate: C = 3J; C - 2 = 4(J-2); 3J - 2 = 4J - 8; 6 = J

11. D. Translate: (3/5)P = M,

$$\frac{\frac{1}{3}M}{P} = \frac{\frac{1}{3}M}{\frac{5}{3}M} =$$

(1/3) X (3/5) = 1/5

12. C. The information, a/4 is an odd integer, gives you the most important information.

13. A. Minimum of m/n occurs when m is minimum and n is maximum. This is when m = .01 and n = 100. So minimum of m/n = .01/100 = 0.0001

14. C. Shaded area = large circle area - small circle area $= \pi a^2 - \pi(\frac{a}{2})^2$

$$= \pi a^2 - \frac{\pi a^2}{4} = \frac{3\pi a^2}{4}$$

15. C. Unshaded area = area of rectangle - area of four squares = ba - 4c²

16. A. Shaded area = area of ½ of circle - area of triangle.

$$= \frac{\pi(\overline{OD})^2}{4} - \frac{(\overline{OD})^2}{2} = \frac{\pi 4^2}{4} - \frac{4^2}{2} = 4\pi - 8$$

17. B. B = 3 X 3 = 9; A = B - area of 3 of the triangles.

So $A = B - \frac{1 \times 2 + 1 \times 1 + 3 \times 1}{2} = 9 - 3 = 6$;

$$\frac{A}{B} = \frac{6}{9} = \frac{2}{3}$$

18. E. You are asked to find speed in kilometers per hour. You must divide minutes by 60 to get hours. So m minutes = m/60 hours.

19. B. $\frac{150}{\frac{x}{60}} = \frac{3000}{y}$ $y = \frac{3000}{150} \times \frac{x}{60} = \frac{x}{3}$

20. E. Let distance uphill (or downhill) = 60 miles. (We choose this number because it can be evenly divided by both 20 and 30). Uphill time, then = 60/20 = 3 hours. Downhill time = 60/30 = 2 hours. Total time is then 5 hours. Total distance is 60 + 60 = 120 miles. So Average Rate = Total distance/total time = 120/5 = 24 mph.

21. A. Sum of scores/12 = 70

$$\frac{\text{Sum of scores} - (\text{three highest and three lowest})}{6}$$

= 64

Separate this last expression:

$$\frac{\text{Sum of scores}}{6} - \frac{\text{three highest and three lowest}}{6}$$

= 64

Average of scores eliminated=

$$\frac{\text{the three highest + three lowest}}{6}$$

$$= \frac{\text{sum of scores}}{6} - 64$$

Now sum of scores/12 = 70, so sum of scores/6 = 140

140 - 64 = 76

22. B. Sum of scores/20 = t

Sum of 15 papers/15 = 70 (Although you don't really need to use this figure)

$$\frac{\text{Sum of 15 papers + sum of 5 papers}}{20} = t$$

$$\frac{\text{Sum of 15 papers}}{20} + \frac{\text{sum of 5 papers}}{20} = t$$

$$\begin{cases} \text{greatest} = 100 \times 5/20 = 500/20 \\ \text{least} = 0 \times 5/20 = 0 \end{cases}$$

greatest - least = 500/20 - 0 = 500/20 = 25

23. A. To get the lowest score on the next text John will have to score 100 on each of the last two tests. So:

$$\frac{60 + 70 + x + 100 + 100}{5} = 70; \quad 330 + x = 350;$$

x = 20

For 24-27--<u>Don't</u> solve for individual variables first! Try to find value of a complete expression directly.

24. D. Start by squaring both sides of the first equation; then expand out the expression $(y + \frac{1}{y})^2$:

$(y + \frac{1}{y})^2 = 9 \times 9 = 81; \quad y^2 + \frac{1}{y^2} + 2 = 81;$

$y^2 + \frac{1}{y^2} = 79.$

25. D. $a + b = c; \quad a - b = \frac{2}{c}; \quad (a + b)(a-b) =$
$a^2 - b^2 = \frac{2}{c} \times c = 2$

26. A. $4m - n = 9$

   $\underline{-(2m - 3n = 5)}$
   $2m + 2n = 4$ $m + n = 2$

27. B. $7a + 4b = 21$

   $\underline{+2a + 2b = 9}$
   $9a + 6b = 30$ $\frac{9a + 6b}{15} = \frac{30}{15} = 2$

28. C. $\frac{a + b}{ab} = \frac{a}{ab} + \frac{b}{ab} = \frac{1}{b} + \frac{1}{a}$

Minimum occurs when b and a are maximum.

So max of $\frac{1}{b} + \frac{1}{a}$ is $\frac{1}{12} + \frac{1}{11}$ (since $12 \geqq b > a$ and b and a are integers)

$$\frac{1}{12} + \frac{1}{11} = \frac{12 + 11}{12 \times 11} = \frac{23}{132}$$

29. B. $30 \times 4000 = 12 \times 10^4$. Thus x = 4.

30. C. $2^6 \times 5^7 = (2 \times 5)^6 \times 5^1$. Thus p = 6.

31. D. $(3^4 - 3^5)(3^2 - 3) = 3^4(3^0 - 3^1)(3^2 - 3)$

$$= 3^4 (1 - 3) (6)$$

$$= 3^4 (-2) (6) = -3^4(12)$$

Note: 32,33,34 require simple substitution.

32. C. $\boxed{\frac{1}{4}} - \boxed{\frac{1}{3}} - \boxed{\frac{1}{15}} = \frac{\frac{1}{4} \times \frac{1}{3}}{\frac{1}{15}} = \frac{\frac{1}{12}}{\frac{1}{15}} = \frac{1}{12} \times 15 = \frac{5}{4}$

33. C. $(1,2,3 \oplus -1,-2,-3) = \frac{1}{-1} + \frac{2}{-2} + \frac{3}{-3}$

$(1,4,1 \oplus 1,2,1) = \frac{1}{1} + \frac{4}{2} + \frac{1}{1}$

Product: $(1,2,3 \oplus -1,-2,-3) \times (1,4,1 \oplus 1,2,1)$
$= (\frac{1}{-1} + \frac{2}{-2} + \frac{3}{-3}) \times (\frac{1}{1} + \frac{4}{2} + \frac{1}{1})$

$= (-3) \times 4 = -12$

34. E. I is correct.

II: $\frac{-\frac{b}{a}}{ } = -(\frac{b+a}{b-a}) = +\frac{a+b}{a-b}$; II is correct.

III. $\frac{\frac{1}{a}}{\frac{1}{b}} = \frac{\frac{1}{a} + \frac{1}{b}}{\frac{1}{a} - \frac{1}{b}} = \frac{\frac{b+a}{ab}}{\frac{b-a}{ab}} = \frac{b+a}{b-a} = -\frac{a}{b}$

III is correct.

35. D. Get rid of fractions:

   $5b = 2c$
   $3f = 2b$
   $4c = d$
   $d = 3e$ } → 3e = d = 4c
   $4c = 3a$ → 4c = 3a, so 3a = 3e; a = e

36. A. $\frac{3}{4} A = 12; \quad A = 16.$ Note: You do not need to use the fact that you are working with an <u>equilateral</u> triangle.

157

Answers to Quantitative Comparison Questions

1-3 Cross out common terms:

1. C. Cross out the a's. c=b because vertical angles are equal.

2. A. Cross out the 54^2 and the 7^3. We are left with
$$(7)(9)(81) > -(7)(9)(81)$$

3. B. Cross out the m^2's. We are left with $0 < 1$.

4. A. Square both sides:
$$(\sqrt{6} + \sqrt{13})^2 \qquad (\sqrt{19})^2$$
$$6 + 13 + \text{other term} > 19$$

5. A. Square both sides:
$$(\sqrt{0.005})^2 \qquad (0.05)^2$$
$$0.005 \quad > \quad 0.0025$$

6. B. Multiply GIVEN $3x + 2 = n$ by 20 to get $60x + 40 = 20n$. Now substitute $20n = 60x + 40$ for Column B. Note, you can also <u>divide</u> both columns by 20 to get $3x + 1$ and n in the Columns and then compare $3x+1$ with n.

7. A. Get rid of common terms. Cross out 2176 to get
$$1/31 \quad > \quad 1/62$$

8. A. Get rid of common terms: Cross out 7,968 to get $5.0 > 4.9$

9. A. Work with addition, not subtraction: add x to both columns to get:

Column A	Column B
x	1

You can see that $x > 1$ from the diagram.

10. A. Work with addition, not subtraction. Add 3b to both columns to get:

Column A	Column B
a + 3b	0

You can see that $a + 3b > 0$

11. A. Work with multiplication instead of with division. First add
$$\frac{1}{400} + \frac{1}{400} = \frac{2}{400}.$$

Then multiply both columns by 400 to get:

Column A	Column B
.2 X .2 X 400	2

You can see that Column A > Column B.

12. B. Work with multiplication instead of division. Multiply both columns by b + c:

Column A	Column B
a	(b+c)d

You get

Column A	Column B
a	bd + cd

But bd + cd > a from GIVEN.

13. C. Translate: a percent of b = c:
$$\frac{a}{100} b = c; \quad ab/c = 100.$$ You can see that Column A = Column B.

14. C. Divide given by 2: 13% of 2x = 120
13% of x = 60

You can see that Column A = Column B.

15-17 Use equal-not equal method to show that Choice D is correct in the following.

15. D. Let x=2, y=2 (equal) (this satisfies Given). Now let x = 1, y = 2 (not equal). So a relationship cannot be determined.

16. D. Let a = 0, b = 0 (equal) (satisfies Given); Let a = 0, b = 2 (not equal) (satisfies Given). Definite relationship cannot be determined.

17. D. a = b (equal); a = -b (not equal). Definite relationship cannot be determined.

18. A. Divide both columns by a (note comparison is now <u>reversed</u> since a is negative). We get

Column A	Column B
$\frac{1}{b}$	b

Now multiply by b: We get:

Column A	Column B
1	b^2

Since $b > 1$, $b^2 > 1$. But since comparison was <u>reversed</u>, original Column A > Column B.

19. D. Use extremes: If m = 100, Column A Column B. If m = 1, Column A Column B. Choice D is therefore correct.

20. D. Since $a < 0$, $bc < 0$ since $abc > 0$. b could be negative and c positive <u>or</u> b could be positive and c negative. Thus a relationship cannot be determined.

21-24--Use equal-unequal method to show Choice D is correct in each of the following:

21. D. m=0, n=0 makes the columns equal. m=2, n=1 makes them unequal. Thus comparison cannot be determined.

22. D. a=4 makes columns equal. a=1 makes them unequal.

23. D. a=1, b=3 makes columns equal. a=6, b=½ makes them unequal.

24. D. a=1, b=2, c=3 makes columns equal. a=1, b=1, c=1 makes them unequal.

25. D. Simplify Given first: $4x<12$, $5y<10$. Divide by common factors. We get: $x<3$ $y<2$. You can see now that Column A Column B if y=1 and x=2. Column A<Column B if y=1 and x=0. So a definite relationship cannot be made.

26. D. Use extremes: If $m = -½$, $m>\frac{1}{m}$, since

$$-½ > \frac{1}{-½} = -2$$

If $m = +½$, $m<\frac{1}{m}$, since $½ < \frac{1}{½} = 2$

A definite comparison cannot be made.

27-32--All questions have columns which involve specific numbers, questions which involve straight calculations, or substitutions without apparent shortcuts. Thus Choice C is likely to be correct in each.

27. C.

28. C.

29. C.

30. C.

31. C.

32. C.